# Learning to Program
# with Alice—Brief Edition

# Learning to Program with Alice— Brief Edition

## Wanda Dann
Ithaca College

## Stephen Cooper
Saint Joseph's University

## Randy Pausch
Carnegie Mellon University

PEARSON
Prentice Hall

Upper Saddle River, NJ 07458

Library of Congress Cataloging-in-Publication Data

Dann, Wanda.
    Learning to program with Alice (Brief) / Wanda Dann, Stephen Cooper, Randy Pausch.
        p.cm.
    ISBN 0-13-239775-7
    1. Alice (Electronic resource : Carnegie-Mellon University. Stage3 Research Group) 2.
Object-oriented programming (Computer science) 3. Computer animation. 4.
Three-dimensional display systems. I. Cooper, Stephen. II. Pausch, Randy. III. Title.

QA76.64.D36 2006
005.1'17--dc22                                                      200647477

Vice President and Editorial Director, ECS: *Marcia J. Horton*
Executive Editor: *Tracy Dunkelberger*
Assistant Editor: *Carole Snyder*
Editorial Assistant: *Christianna Lee*
Executive Managing Editor: *Vince O'Brien*
Managing Editor: *Camille Trentacoste*
Production Editor: *Donna Crilly*
Director of Creative Services: *Paul Belfanti*
Creative Director: *Juan Lopez*
Art Director: *Kenny Beck*
Cover Designer: *Kenny Beck*
Director, Image Resource Center: *Melinda Reo*
Manager, Rights and Permissions: *Zina Arabia*
Manager, Visual Research: *Beth Brenzel*
Manager, Cover Visual Research & Permissions: *Karen Sanatar*
Image Permission Coordinator: *Angelique Sharps*
Manufacturing Manager: *Alexis Heydt-Long*
Manufacturing Buyer: *Lisa McDowell*
Executive Marketing Manager: *Robin O'Brien*
Marketing Assistant: *Mack Patterson*
Cover Photo: *Susan Seubert / Botanica / Getty Images, Inc.*

© 2007 Pearson Education, Inc.
Pearson Prentice Hall
Pearson Education, Inc.
Upper Saddle River, NJ 07458

Printed in the United States of America
10  9  8  7  6  5  4  3  2  1

ISBN 0-13-239775-7

Pearson Education Ltd., *London*
Pearson Education Australia Pty. Ltd., *Sydney*      Pearson Educación de Mexico, S.A. de C.V.
Pearson Education Singapore, Pte. Ltd.               Pearson Education—Japan, *Tokyo*
Pearson Education North Asia Ltd., *Hong Kong*       Pearson Education Malaysia Pte. Ltd.
Pearson Education Canada Inc., *Toronto*             Pearson Education, Inc., *Upper Saddle River, New Jersey*

To Brian, Wendy, Jerry, and Noah
*Wanda Dann*

To Sandi and Jeanna
*Stephen Cooper*

To Jai, Dylan, Logan, and Chloe
*Randy Pausch*

# Contents

# Appendix   101

# Foreword

Introductory programming has always been a frustrating course for many students, and recent attempts to include object-oriented programming in the first semester have only compounded an already difficult learning experience. This is especially worrisome when recent surveys show a 23% decline in the number of CS majors. We simply can't afford to discourage students by needlessly frustrating them in their first exposure to computing.

The Alice system represents a breakthrough in teaching object-oriented computing: in Alice, objects are easily visible, because they are reified as three-dimensional humans, animals, furniture, etc. The state of Alice objects is changed via method calls such as "move forward one meter" or "turn left a quarter turn"—these messages are easily and intuitively understood by students. Computation is displayed via animations of these state changes: one can hardly imagine a more visceral way to express the notion of embodying state in an object and using computation to change that state. One of Alice's real strengths is that it has been able to make abstract concepts concrete in the eyes of first-time programmers.

Any good teacher knows that if a student is not motivated to learn, all the pedagogy and technique in the world won't help: students learn best when they are internally motivated. While we can create that motivation via rewards and punishments (i.e. "grades") the Alice system uses a purer form of motivation: it bases programming in the activity of storytelling which is universally compelling: as we say in Los Angeles, "everybody wants to direct."

By using 3D graphics as the authoring medium, the Alice system speaks directly to a generation raised on videogames and PIXAR's films; the authors leverage that by using "storyboarding" as a metaphor for computer program design—storyboarding being one of the few "design activities" that can be immediately understood by a college freshman.

Coupled with the high-level concepts such as reifying objects, the Alice system provides a well-engineered drag-and-drop user interface, inspired by the Squeak system's editor, that allows students to drag program components around the screen and guarantees that the student cannot make a syntax error.

One could make the argument that Alice is one of the most novel systems to hit introductory computing in the last twenty years—and it's arriving just in time!

ALAN KAY

*Dr. Kay is one of the earliest pioneers of object-oriented programming, personal computing and graphical user interfaces. His contributions have been recognized with the Charles Stark Draper Prize of the National Academy of Engineering (with Robert Taylor, Butler Lampson, and Charles Thacker), the A.M. Turing Award from the Association of Computing Machinery, and the Kyoto Prize from the Inamori Foundation.*

# Preface

*"...what is the use of a book," thought Alice, "without pictures or conversation?"*

This book and the associated Alice system take an innovative approach to introductory programming. There have been relatively few innovations in the teaching of programming in the last 30 years, even though such courses are often extremely frustrating to students. The goal of our innovative approach is to allow traditional programming concepts to be more easily taught and more readily understood. The Alice system is free and is available at www.alice.org.

## What should a programming course teach?

While many people have strong opinions on this topic, we feel there is a strong consensus that a student in a programming course should learn the following:

- Algorithmic thinking and expression: being able to read and write in a formal language.
- Abstraction: learning how to communicate complex ideas simply and to decompose problems logically.
- Appreciation of elegance: realizing that although there are many ways to solve a problem, some are inherently better than others.

## What is different about our approach?

Our approach allows students to author on-screen movies and games, in which the concept of an "object" is made tangible and visible. In Alice, on-screen objects populate a 3D micro world. Students create programs by dragging and dropping program elements (if/then statements, loops, variables, etc.) in a mouse-based editor that prohibits syntax errors. The Alice system provides a powerful, modern programming environment that supports methods, functions, variables, parameters, recursion, arrays, and events. We use this strong visual environment to support either an objects-first or an objects-early approach (described in the ACM and IEEE-CS Computing Curricula 2001 report) with an early introduction to events. In Alice, every object is an object that students can visibly see! We introduce objects in the very first chapter.

In our opinion, four primary obstacles to introductory programming must be overcome:

1. **The fragile mechanics of program creation, particularly syntax** The Alice editing environment removes the frustration of syntax errors in program creation and allows students to develop an intuition for syntax, because every time a program element is dragged into the editor, all valid "drop targets" are highlighted.

2. **The inability to see the results of computation as the program runs** Although textual debuggers and variable watchers are better than nothing, the Alice approach makes the state of the program inherently visible. In a sense, we offload the mental effort from the student's cognitive system to his or her perceptual system. It is much easier for a student to see that an object has moved backward instead of forward than to notice that the "sum" variable has been decremented, rather than incremented. Alice allows students to see how their animated programs run, affording an easy relationship of the program construct to the animation action. Today's students are immersed in a world where interactive, three-dimensional graphics are commonplace; we try to leverage that fact without pandering to them.

3. **The lack of motivation for programming** Many students take introductory programming courses only because they are required to do so. Nothing will ever be more motivating than a stellar teacher, but the right environment can go a long way. In pilot studies of classes using Alice, students do more optional exercises and are more likely to take a second class in programming than control groups of students using traditional tools. The most common request we received regarding earlier versions of Alice was to be able to share creations with peers; we have added the ability to run Alice programs in a World Wide Web browser so students can post them on their Web pages. Although we have seen increased motivation for all students, we have seen especially encouraging results with underrepresented groups, especially female students.

4. **The difficulty of understanding compound logic and learning design techniques** The Alice environment physically encourages the creation of small methods and functions. More importantly, the analogy of making a movie allows us to utilize the concept of a storyboard, which students recognize as an established movie-making process. We illustrate design techniques using simple sketches and screen captures. Also, we encourage the use of textual storyboards, progressively refining them and essentially designing with pseudocode.

## How to use this text

Of course, as an instructor, you should use this text as you see fit! We list two ways we imagine the book being used, but you may discover others:

**As the first portion of a traditional "Introduction to Programming" course**, such as CS1. Both Seymour Papert's Logo and Rich Pattis' Karel the Robot have been used this way, and these systems have inspired us greatly. Unlike these systems, Alice is powerful enough to support students for several semesters (for example, seniors majoring in computer science at Carnegie Mellon routinely write 3,000-line programs in Alice). However, many introductory programming courses must both teach concepts and also prepare students to write programs in traditional languages, such as Java. By learning Alice first, students become acquainted with the fundamental concepts of programming, and can quickly learn the specific syntax rules of a particular "real" language as a transition.

**As the programming component of a "Computer Literacy" course.** At many schools, computer literacy courses attempt to give non-majors a broad introduction to computers and/or "information technology." Many of these courses have removed their programming component and are little more than extended laboratories on "office productivity tools" such as spreadsheets and word processors. Alice has the potential to return a gentle programming component to computer literacy courses.

## Instructional materials

An errata list, lecture notes, links to other instructional materials, and examples of course schedules can be found at http://www.aliceprogramming.net.

## Structure of the book

Chapter 1 gives students some motivating reasons to want to write a computer program and addresses any fears they may have about programming (especially helpful for computer literacy courses). It then introduces some basic Alice concepts. A traditional, paper-based tutorial is presented in Appendix A. Computing and programming terminology (e.g., program, class, and object) are written in blue when first introduced and defined.

The remaining chapters each begin with a motivational overview of the chapter's topic and end with exercises, projects, and a summary. The list below is a (very) brief overview of the major concepts covered, chapter by chapter. Clearly, the major focus of the text material is to introduce the fundamental concepts of programming.

Each chapter has a "Tips & Techniques" section. Collectively, these sections and Appendices A and B comprise a mini User's Guide to Alice. The Tips & Techniques cover animation in Alice rather than traditional fundamental concepts of programming presented in the major chapter material. The techniques explained in these sections are strategically placed throughout the text, laying the groundwork for using these techniques in programming examples that follow. Tips & Techniques provide a guide for those who want to learn more about animation with Alice. Appendix A is a "getting started" tutorial. Appendix B describes how to manage the interface. Use of the interface is also integrated with text examples for programming concepts, where needed. The Tips & Techniques sections enrich the flavor of the book with selected "how to" topics.

## Topic selection and sequence of coverage

The topic selection and sequence of coverage is in the instructor's hands!

In working with instructors in various college and university settings, we found that topic selection and sequences are often based on time constraints for a particular course structure, pedagogy, and philosophy of teaching. If you are limited to three or four weeks as part of a larger course, you may wish to assign exercises throughout with only one project at the end. Also, you can use Tips & Techniques sections as reading assignments, not requiring classroom presentation time.

## Notes concerning specific aspects of the text

If you are using this text to teach/learn Alice without discussing design, you may skip the first section of Chapter 2. However, textual storyboards and stepwise refinement will be used throughout the rest of the text to provide a framework in which to discuss design from an algorithmic, problem-solving perspective. You may choose to use a different design framework (perhaps the Unified Modeling Language or a more traditional version of pseudocode). This may be done safely, without impacting the content.

In Chapter 4, we note that Alice does not provide a complete implementation of inheritance. When a new class is created in Alice, it gets a copy of the properties and methods of the base class and is saved in a new 3D model file. Subsequent changes to the super class are not reflected in the subclass.

## Alice

The latest version of the Alice software and online galleries of 3D models can be downloaded from http://www.alice org. The version of Alice on the disk supplied with this book is meant to run on a PC with the Windows ME, 2000, or XP operating system. If you are using a Macintosh or a PC with Linux, check the Web site http://www.alice.org for a version of Alice compatible with your system. The Alice website also provides instructions for installation, Frequently Asked Questions, links for receiving bug reports, and access to an online community forum for Alice educators.

The Alice system is 3D graphics and memory intensive. The Alice development team has a set of minimum and recommended requirements for running Alice. Please note that many older laptops do not meet these requirements. It is extremely important to try Alice on the specific machines you will be using, just to be sure.

**Operating system requirements:**

Windows ME, 2000, or XP

**Minimum hardware requirements:**

A Pentium running at 500 MHz or better

VGA graphics card capable of high (16 bit) color

128 MB of RAM

Video resolution of $1024 \times 768$

A sound card

**Recommended hardware requirements:**

A Pentium running at 1.0 GHz or better

16 MB 3D video card (see www.alice.org for more details)

256 MB of RAM

Alice works well with digital projection systems for classroom demonstrations. Projectors limited to $800 \times 600$ video resolution will work, although $1024 \times 768$ is best.

## Acknowledgments

As noted above, Seymour Papert's Logo and Rich Pattis' Karel the Robot were great inspirations in using a visible micro world. Alan Kay and the Squeak team inspired us to create the mouse-based program editor, and we were also inspired by the syntax-directed editor work done by Tim Teitelbaum. We are indebted to George Polya, Mike Clancy, and Doug Cooper for our problem-solving approach.

Our deep gratitude goes to early testers and users of our text and instructional materials for their helpful comments and suggestions: Susan Rodger (Duke University), Rick Zaccone (Bucknell University), Bill Taffe (Plymouth State), Angela Shifflet (Wofford College), and William Taylor (Camden County College). In addition, we are thankful for the assistance of our students: Toby Dragon (Ithaca College), Kevin Dietzler (Saint Joseph's University), Patricia Hasson (Saint Joseph's University), and Kathleen Ryan (Saint Joseph's University).

The life and breath of the Alice software is dependent on a group of creative, energetic, and dedicated graduate students, undergraduate students, and staff members at Carnegie Mellon University. Without these people, Alice does not live and we could not have written this textbook. The primary authors of this version of Alice include Ben Buchwald, Dennis Cosgrove, Dave Culyba, Cliff Forlines, Jason Pratt, and Caitlin Kelleher; a more complete list is available at www.alice.org. Many artists at Carnegie Mellon have graciously placed their work into the gallery for the benefit of others. We list Sarah Hatton, Mo Mahler, Shawn Lawson and Tiffany Pomarico here, but the contributors run into the hundreds. Tommy Burnette, Kevin Christiansen, Rob Deline, Matt Conway, and Rich Gossweiller all made seminal contributions to earlier versions of Alice at the University of Virginia. We also thank the University for its support and encouragement of earlier versions of Alice.

This material is based upon work partially supported by the National Science Foundation under Grant Numbers 0302542, 0339734, and 0126833. Any opinions, findings, and conclusions or recommendations expressed in this material are those of the author(s) and do not necessarily reflect the views of the National Science Foundation.

We also thank the reviewers, who provided valuable comments and suggestions:

John Dougherty, Haverford College
Mark Guzdial, Georgia Institute of Technology
Susan Rodger, Duke University
Rick Zaccone, Bucknell University
Mary Ann Amy-Pumphrey, De Anza College

Richard Pattis, Carnegie Mellon University
Deb Deppeler, University of Wisconsin
Odis Hayden Griffin, Jr., Virginia Tech
William Taylor, Camden County College
Suzanne Westbrook, University of Arizona
Kendra Dinerstein, Utah State University
Leland Beck, San Diego State University
Elizabeth Boese, Colorado State University
Sally Peterson, University of Wisconsin

We thank Tracy Dunkelberger of Prentice Hall and Alan Apt for supporting this effort. Over the last ten years DARPA, NASA, Apple, Ford, Intel, Microsoft Research, and SAIC have contributed support for the development of the Alice system, for which we are most grateful.

WANDA DANN
STEPHEN COOPER
RANDY PAUSCH

# Part I
# Introduction to Alice

# Chapter 1

# Getting Started with Alice

*"Let's pretend there's a way of getting through into it, somehow, Kitty. Let's pretend the glass has got all soft like gauze, so that we can get through. Why, it's turning into a sort of mist now, I declare! It'll be easy enough to get through—"*

## 1-1 Introduction to Alice

### Why learn about programming computers?

We are guessing that you are reading this book because either (a) you **want to learn about programming** computers, or (b) **you are taking a course where you are required** to learn about programming computers. In either case, let's begin by talking about why it might be valuable for you to learn how to write computer programs.

First, let's get one thing out of the way: **learning to program a computer does not turn you into a computer nerd**. We know there are lots of preformed ideas in people's heads about what computer programming is, and what kinds of people write computer programs. But we promise that you won't suddenly develop a desire to wear a pocket protector, stop taking showers, or start speaking in obscure computer-language abbreviations. Honest. **This book uses a system called Alice, which makes it possible to write computer programs in a totally different way than ever before**. Rather than typing obscure "computer language" into a machine in the hopes of getting it to do some sort of strange calculation, you'll have the opportunity to be the director of a play, where on-screen objects act out the script you create! But let's not get too far ahead of ourselves. Let's get back to why you might want to program a computer at all.

There are many reasons to learn to program a computer. For some people, computer programming is actually a great deal of fun—they enjoy it as an end unto itself. But for most people, writing computer programs is satisfying because it is a means to an end; they have something important to do, and the computer is a useful tool for them. In fact, the applications of computers are becoming so pervasive in our society that if you were born tomorrow you might be interacting with a computer from your very first day to your very last. Many hospitals put a small computer chip on a band around your ankle as a newborn, to make sure they know where you are at all times. On your last day, you are likely to have a computer monitoring your vital signs on your deathbed. In between, you're likely to live a lot longer and a lot healthier, because of computer advances aiding medical research, computer-controlled brakes and airbags in our cars, and computer modeling that allows us to design new drugs to fight

3

diseases like AIDS. Computer programmers help to make all of these technological advances possible.

Computers, and the software that computer programmers write for them, have revolutionized the entertainment industry. Computer gaming is becoming increasingly popular. The Pew Internet and American Life Project reported (in 2003) that about 70 percent of college students play online computer games at least once a week. Movies in the *Star Wars* series, and the special effects in them, are only possible because of computers. By the way, one of the undergraduate authors of the Alice system graduated and went to work at ILM (Industrial Light and Magic), who do the special effects for *Star Wars* films. So the next time you watch *The Phantom Menace*, look for Tommy Burnette in the credits!

Computers help us communicate with each other by maintaining complex cellular telephone networks, they aid marine research by tracking animal migratory patterns, and they allow us to explore space. None of these things would be possible without computers.

Of course, many of the people who write the software for these projects are professionals who have spent years studying programming. But even people who are not planning to be professionals can benefit greatly from even a single course in programming. Modern applications, like spreadsheets and word processors, give end users the opportunity to save time and effort by using "macros" or other programming-like features that tell the computer to do something long and tedious, instead of having the user do it. Also, if you have even a little experience with programming, you're much more likely to become the "go to" person in an office where computers are used, which can help you get ahead in your career.

Most importantly, even one course in computer programming can be useful as a way of **learning a new way to think**, much as taking a drawing course is a way to learn how to **look at the world differently**. Learning to think in new ways is always extremely valuable. Many of us talk about how we'd like to improve our general problem-solving skills. "Problem solving" is really just finding an answer to a question or figuring out how to perform a task. Computer programming is a pure, distilled form of problem solving. So, learning to program a computer will truly help you learn a new way to think—enabling you to find answers to questions and figure out how to make things work.

## How you will learn to program with this book and Alice

This book and the associated Alice system will teach you to program a computer, but in a fundamentally different and more enjoyable way than ever before. In terms of tone, we have worked very hard to make learning to program as painless as humanly possible. Most programming, especially in introductory computing courses, has the feeling of mundane calculation: add up a bunch of numbers, and print out their sum and average. Often, students find these courses frustrating because of all the obscure technical details they must get right before anything will work at all. Students often talk about singing songs in ritual attempts to appease the computer gods. We felt there had to be a better way.

This book uses a completely different approach that is only recently possible due to the increased power of desktop computers and the development of novel software that uses that power, especially for 3D graphics. The Alice system, which is provided freely as a public service by Carnegie Mellon University,[1] provides a completely new approach to learning to program. Originally developed as part of a research project in Virtual Reality,[2] Alice lets you be the director of a movie, or the creator of a video game, where 3D objects in an on-screen virtual world move around according to the directions you give them. Rather than using obscure computer terms, you use natural English language words, like "move forward" or "turn right." Best of all, you can't make mistakes! Well, of course you can **always** make some mistakes,

---

[1]We also gratefully thank the University of Virginia, where an earlier version of Alice was developed.

[2]We gratefully acknowledge the support of the National Science Foundation, DARPA, Intel, and a number of other sponsors who have supported the Alice project: a complete list is available at www.alice.org.

such as telling one of your objects to move forward when you **meant** to move it backward. You can't, however, make the kind of "computer mistake" that most students get frustrated by—where you type something wrong and you can't figure out why the program won't run at all.

If the term "computer programmer" makes you think of some poor drudge hunched over a computer keyboard in a darkened room—don't worry! You'll almost never even touch the keyboard when using the Alice system. You will create programs by dragging words and objects around on the screen using the mouse. Then, when you press the **"Play"** button (circled in Figure 1-1-1), the objects in the 3D world on your screen will come to life and act out the script you have written for them! So, in a sense, **being a "computer programmer" using Alice is really like being a movie director, a puppeteer, or a choreographer**—anyone who gives people instructions about what to do in a precise but limited vocabulary.

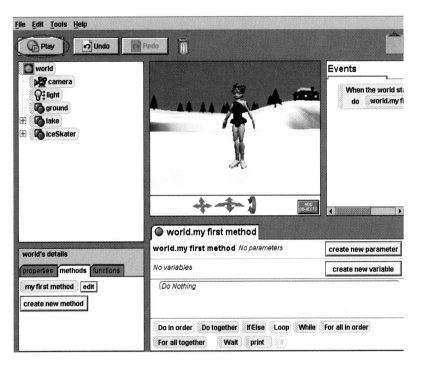

**Figure 1-1-1.** An Alice 3D World

**After you've learned how to use Alice, you'll understand all the fundamental ideas involved in programming**. Then, you will be in great shape to use one of the "real world" languages where you have to type with the keyboard and get all the commas and semicolons in the right place. You will know how to program, and all you'll have to learn are the particular grammar "rules" (sometimes called the "syntax"[3]) of languages like Java, C++, C#, or whatever.

## The basics of computer programming

A computer program is really nothing more than a set of instructions that tell the computer what to do. Of course, there are many ways of telling the computer to do something, so how you do it can matter. Believe it or not, computer programmers often use words like "elegant" to describe well-written programs. We recommend that you think of a computer program not

---

[3]Not to be confused with *sin tax*, a tax on things like cigarettes or alcohol.

only as a way to tell the computer what to do, but also as a way to tell another human being what you want the computer to do.

A computer program is not only "a way to tell the computer what to do."

A computer program is a way to tell another human being what you want the computer to do.

That makes it a lot easier to talk about whether something is "elegant." A program is elegant if other human beings can easily understand and appreciate the intentions of the original programmer. For this reason, one basic part of writing a computer program is to include documentation (comments in the program, a web page for reference, or an accompanying written document) that helps another human being understand what you were trying to do.

The key to computer programming is to get a handle on the fundamental ideas. At its heart, programming is really very simple. All computer programs are made from very simple ideas:

**A list of instructions:** For example, "Beat eggs, mix in flour, sugar, and shortening, pour into baking pan, then bake at 375 degrees for 45 minutes." Computer scientists call this sequential processing.

**Ifs:** For example, "IF it is raining, take an umbrella." Computer scientists call this conditional execution.

**Repeating behavior:** For example, "Stomp your foot five times" or "WHILE there are cookies on the plate, keep eating cookies." (That last part actually sounded kind of fun!) Computer scientists call this looping, or iteration.

**Breaking things up into smaller pieces:** For example, "The way we're going to clean the house is to first clean the kitchen, then clean the bathroom, then clean each of the three bedrooms one at a time." Okay, so that doesn't sound like as much fun as eating the cookies, but it's still a pretty easy concept. Computer scientists call this problem decomposition, or stepwise refinement, or top-down design, but it's really an ancient philosophical approach called reductionism. Regardless of what you call it, it means that to do a complicated task, break it down into a list of simpler tasks. The result of accomplishing all the simpler tasks is that the complicated task is accomplished.

**Compute a result:** Here we perform a sequence of steps to obtain a result that is an answer to a question. For example, "Look in the phone book and find the number for Rebecca Smith," or "Put this baby on a scale and tell me how many pounds she weighs." Actually, each of these actions embodies a question: "What is Rebecca's phone number?" or "How much does the baby weigh?" A question is known as a function in computer programming. Asking a question so as to compute a result (find an answer) is known as calling a function.

Computer programming is really just using these ideas in various combinations. What can make things hard is complexity. The truth is that most computers "understand" only about 100 different instructions. The millions of programs that run on computers use these same 100 instructions in different orders and combinations. So where is the complexity? Think about it like this: In a chess game, there are only six kinds of chess pieces, and each piece moves in a simple pattern. Chess is a complicated game because of all the possible combinations of moves.

To put this another way, writing a computer program is like putting on a stage play with 200 actors, 500 costumes, and 5 live camels that appear in Act II, Scene IV. Things can get complicated just because that's a lot to keep track of! This book will teach you some tricks for managing complexity and for planning out how to write programs before you actually try to make them work. In fact, **learning how to think about arranging a sequence of instructions to carry out a task (how to design a program) is probably the most valuable part of learning to program.** You may have heard the term object-oriented programming. This textbook and the Alice system are based on the use of objects. In an Alice program, the objects are things you can actually see.

### Why is it called Alice?

First of all, Alice is not an acronym: it isn't A.L.I.C.E and it doesn't stand for anything. The team named the system "Alice" in honor of Charles Lutwidge Dodson, an English mathematician and logician who wrote under the pen name Lewis Carroll. Carroll wrote *Alice's Adventures in Wonderland* and *Through the Looking Glass*. Just like the people who built Alice, Lewis Carroll was able to do complex mathematics and logic, but he knew that the most important thing was to make things simple and fascinating to a learner.

In the same way that Alice was hesitant when she first stepped through the looking glass, you may have some doubts about learning to program. Please take that first step, and we promise that **learning to program a computer will be easier than you might think**.

## 1-2 Alice concepts

Learning to program in Alice means that you will create virtual worlds on your computer and populate them with some really cool objects in creative scenes. Then, you will write programs (sort of like movie scripts or video game controllers) to direct your own production of animations in those worlds. In this section, we begin with an overview of the Alice software and the interface to help you get started. This section works hand-in-hand with the Getting Started exercises in Appendix A. We suggest that you read this section and work through the Getting Started exercises while sitting at a computer where you can try things out as you read.

### Concept: Virtual world

Video games and simulations can be either two or three dimensional (2D or 3D). You may have used a 2D graphic simulator in a driver education course. Pilots, as part of their training, use flight simulators. The advantage of simulations is obvious—when a fighter plane crashes under the hands of the novice pilot, neither the pilot nor the aircraft is actually in danger. A video game or simulation implemented in 3D is called a virtual world. Using a virtual world lends a sense of reality to the simulator and increases its effectiveness.

To see the difference between 2D and 3D, compare the images in Figures 1-2-1 and 1-2-2. Figure 1-2-1 shows a movie set mock-up front and back. Clearly the structure is 2D because it has width and height, but no depth. Figure 1-2-2 shows front and back camera shots of the tortoise and hare out for their daily exercise run. The tortoise and hare are objects in a 3D virtual world, having width, height, and depth, so camera shots captured from different angles show objects that give a sense of being real.

**Figure 1-2-1.** 2D mock-up, front and back view

**Figure 1-2-2.** 3D world with the tortoise and hare, front and back view

An Alice virtual world begins with a template for an initial scene. The templates are shown in the opening window when Alice is started. The templates can be seen in Figure 1-2-3, where we have selected an initial scene composed of a blue sky and a grassy-green ground surface.

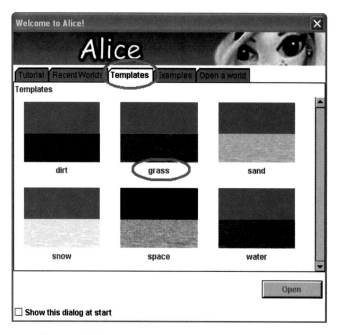

**Figure 1-2-3.** Selecting a template for an initial scene

## Concept: Objects and 3D models

Part of the fun of using Alice is to use your imagination to create new worlds. We begin with a simple scene and add objects. In the world shown in Figure 1-2-2, the objects added are a tree, fence, tortoise and hare. Some objects provide a setting (trees, houses, starry skies, and such). Other objects (people, animals, space ships, and others) play the role of actors in your script (that is, they move around and perform various actions during the animation).

To make it easy to create a new world and populate it with all kinds of objects, the Alice developers have provided a huge number of 3D models. In a way, a 3D model is like a blueprint used to design a house. The blueprint provides a model of what the house will look like, the location and size of each room in the house, and some instructions for the housing contractor to follow in actually building the house. Likewise, an Alice 3D model tells Alice how to create a new object in the scene. The 3D model provides instructions on how to draw the object, what color it should be, what parts it should have, its size (height, width, and depth), and many other details.

The installation of Alice on your computer includes a Local gallery that contains a selection of 3D models. Additional models can be found in the Web gallery (http://www.alice.org) and on the CD provided with this book. Easy access to the 3D models in a gallery collection is provided by the scene editor, shown in Figure 1-2-4. If you have the CD in your CD ROM, a CD gallery folder will also appear in the folder. Examples and exercises in this book use models from both the Local and the Web galleries. If you want to use a 3D model that does not appear in the Local gallery, you can find it on the CD or the Web gallery.

Alice is not a 3D graphics drawing program. This is why generous galleries of 3D models are provided. It is not possible, though, to think of everything someone may want for a virtual world. To help you build people objects of your own, custom builder tools (*hebuilder* and

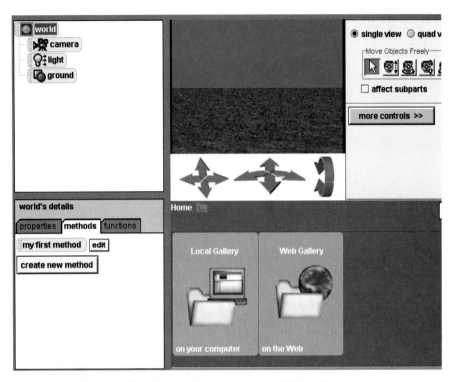

**Figure 1-2-4.** Scene editor with Local and Web gallery folders

*shebuilder)* are available in the People folder of the Local gallery. Details on using these tools are provided in Appendix B.

## Concept: Three dimensions and six directions

Objects in an Alice world are three dimensional. Each object has width, height, and depth, as illustrated in Figure 1-2-5. (In this world, the astronaut has been added (People gallery folder) to the space world template.) The height is measured along an imaginary line running vertically from top to bottom, the width along an imaginary line running horizontally from left to right, and the depth along an imaginary line running from front to back.

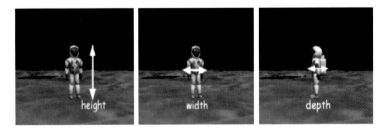

**Figure 1-2-5.** Three dimensions

In terms of these three dimensions, an object "knows" which way is *up* or *down* relative to itself. Also, the object understands the meaning of *left* and *right* and *forward* and *backward*, as seen in Figure 1-2-6. This amounts to six possible directions in which an object may move. That is, an object has six degrees of freedom to move around in a world. It is important to notice, for example, that directions are *left* and *right* with respect to the astronaut object, not the camera's point of view. We call the six degrees of freedom (possible directions of motion) the

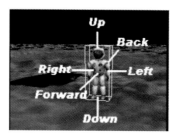

**Figure 1-2-6.** Object orientation: six degrees of freedom

object's orientation. When you mouse-click an object in an Alice world, a yellow bounding box is displayed, as seen in Figure 1-2-6. The bounding box highlights the selected object.

## Concept: Center of an object

Each object in Alice has a unique "center." The center point isn't calculated. Instead, it is a feature of each object that is set by a graphic artist when the 3D model is first created. Usually, the center point of an object is at the center of its bounding box—or as near to the center of mass as the graphic artist could determine. The center point provides a reference for a pivot or spin type of movement. So, an object like a tire or a bird will spin around its center. Figure 1-2-7 illustrates the center of a bird object. We used a wire frame display to show that the center of the bird is located in the interior of its body.

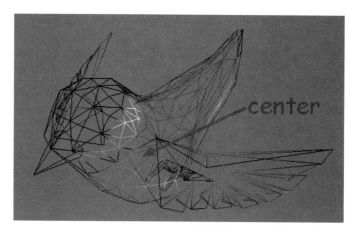

**Figure 1-2-7.** Center at the center of mass

Not all objects have their center located at their center of mass. Those that generally sit or stand on the ground or a table have their center located at the bottom of their bounding box. For people objects, the center point is between their feet, as shown in Figure 1-2-8. This is because a person's feet are on the ground and the distance of the person above the ground is zero (0) meters.

Other kinds of objects that do not have a center at the center of mass are those that are "held" when used, such as a baseball bat. The center point of a baseball bat is where it would be held, as illustrated in Figure 1-2-9. The center is on the handle so that when you rotate it, it will "swing" about that point.

## Concept: Distance

One object's distance to another is measured from its center. For example, the bird's distance downward to the ground in Figure 1-2-10 is measured from the bird's center.

**Figure 1-2-8.**  Center of an object that stands on the ground

**Figure 1-2-9.**  Center of an object that is held

**Figure 1-2-10.**  Distance downward to the ground is measured from the center

## Concept: Position

The center of an object is the point used as its "position" in a world. Alice automatically puts the center of the ground at the center of the world. In Figure 1-2-11, a set of coordinate axes is positioned at the center of the ground. In the properties list for the ground (located in the details panel at the lower left of Figure 1-2-11), you can see that the center of the ground is located at (0, 0, and 0).

Like the ground, any object in the world is located relative to the center of the world. The bird in Figure 1-2-12 is located at position (−3.41, 1.59, 6.15). That is, the center of the bird is 3.41 meters left, 1.59 meters above, and 6.15 meters forward of the center of the world.

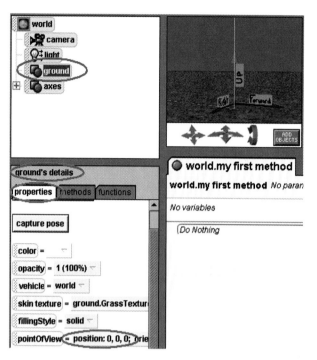

**Figure 1-2-11.** The center of the ground is located at the center of the world

## Concept: Animation

In Alice, you will build virtual worlds and create animations by moving the objects in a world in the same way that objects are moved in a flight simulator or a video game. You will use many of the same techniques to give the illusion of motion as are used by animators to create animated cartoons for film studios such as Disney® and Pixar®. Animation is a fantasy of vision, an illusion. To generate this illusion, the filmmaker and artist collaborate to create a sequence of artwork frames (drawings or images) where each has a slightly different view of a scene. The scene is drawn with objects, and then redrawn with the objects positioned in a slightly different place. The scene is drawn again and the objects moved just a bit more, over and over and over! Figure 1-2-13 illustrates a sequence of frames in Alice.

In animation production, frames are photographed in sequence on a reel of film or captured by a digital video camera. The film is run through a projector or viewed on a monitor, displaying many pictures in rapid sequence and creating an illusion of motion. Alice creates a similar effect on your computer screen. There is no need to worry about being a great artist. Alice takes care of all the computer graphic work to create the sequence of frames. You act as the director to tell Alice what actions the objects are to perform. Alice creates (renders) the animation.

## Getting started with Alice

We encourage you to experiment with the Alice system in much the same way as you would explore a new cell phone. You take it out of the box and try out all its cool features—sort of a "poke and prod" kind of procedure. In the same way, you can learn how to use the Alice system.

Appendix A provides a tutorial-style Getting Started set of self-paced exercises with detailed instructions on how to start a new Alice world, where to find the galleries of 3D models, how to change the color of the ground, and how to add objects to a new world and properly position them in a scene. If you have not already done so, go and do these exercises now!

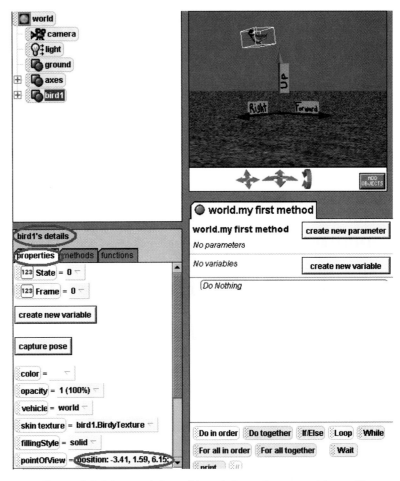

**Figure 1-2-12.** The bird's position relative to the center of the world

**Figure 1-2-13.** A sequence of frames to create an animation

## Tips & Techniques 1
### Special Effects: Text and 2D Graphic Images

While it is beyond the scope of this text to cover all of Alice's special capabilities, we will show you some of its features as we work through examples. At the end of each chapter, Tips & Techniques sections will present fun ways to build great animations with special effects. Although these Tips & Techniques sections are not essential to learning fundamental programming concepts, they are important to read because some of these techniques are used in example worlds. Tips & Techniques provide a guide for those who want to learn more about animation. Additional details of using Alice are also provided in Appendix B, where you can learn how to search the gallery and how to export a world to the Web. The Tips & Techniques sections along with Appendix A and Appendix B can be considered a mini User's Guide for Alice.

An important aspect of an animation is communicating information to the person viewing the animation (the user). Text, sound, and graphic images help you communicate. The following sections show how to add text and graphic images to your world.

### 3D text

To add a 3D text object to a world, click on the Create 3D Text thumbnail in the Local Gallery, as seen in Figure T-1-1.

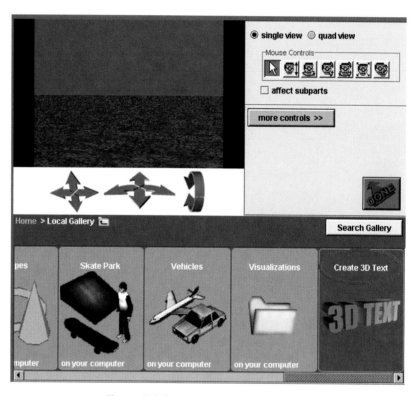

**Figure T-1-1.** 3D text in the Local Gallery

A text dialog box pops up for entering text, as in Figure T-1-2. The dialog box allows font, bold, and italic selections, and a text box where words can be typed.

When the Okay button is clicked, Alice adds a text object to the world and an entry for the object in the Object tree. The name of the object is the same as the text displayed, as seen in Figure T-1-3.

The text object can be positioned using mouse controls in the same way as any other object. To modify the text in the object string, click on the text in the properties list of the details panel. Then, enter a new string of text in the popup dialog box, illustrated in Figure T-1-4.

Note that modifying the string in the text object does not modify the name of the object. The name is still as it was when the text object was originally created, as seen in Figure T-1-5.

**Figure T-1-2.**  A text dialog box

**Figure T-1-3.**  The text object is added to the scene and object tree

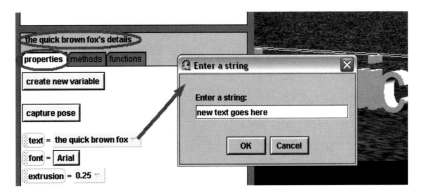

**Figure T-1-4.**  Modifying text

**Figure T-1-5.**  The name of text object remains the same

## Graphic images (Billboards)

Although Alice is a 3D system, it is possible to display flat 2D images in a scene. Flat 2D images can be created in any paint tool and saved in GIF, JPG, or TIF formats. To add a 2D image (Alice calls it a billboard) to your world, select **Make Billboard** from the **Fil**e menu, as seen in Figure T-1-6. In the selection dialog box, navigate to the stored image and then click the **Import** button.

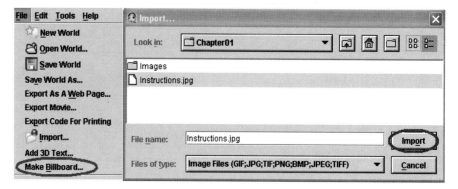

**Figure T-1-6.** Importing a billboard

Alice will add the flat image to the world. The billboard in Figure T-1-7 illustrates one of the uses of billboards—providing information to the user about how to play a game or simulation. In this example, a billboard provides instructions for how to use the keyboard to control the motion of an object. (Keyboard control examples are used in Chapter 5.)

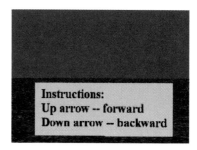

**Figure T-1-7.** A billboard to provide information

## Exercises

The exercises below are to verify that you have learned and are comfortable using the Alice software. The goal in each exercise is to create an initial scene for a world. Alice will periodically prompt you to save your world. (Instructions on how to save a world are provided in the Getting Started exercises in Appendix A.) A name for your world is suggested by the name of the exercise. For example, the world in Exercise 1 could be named *Island.a2w*.

**The objects in each world are created from the 3D models in the Alice gallery. Most models are located in the Local Gallery included in the Alice installation. If the model is not in the Local gallery, look for the model in the CD gallery or the online Web gallery (www.alice.org).**

1. *Island*
   Create an island scene. Start by choosing a water world template. (Alternatively, start with a green grass world and change the ground color to *blue*.) Add an island object (from the Environments gallery folder). Use the scene editor to position the island a bit to the right of the center of the scene. Now, add a goldfish to the scene. You may find that the goldfish is invisible because it is located behind the island or is not properly positioned. Use the scene editor and its quad view to arrange the goldfish so it looks like it is swimming in the water to the left of the island. Use the camera controls to zoom out so the island and the goldfish are both in the camera's view.

2. *Winter*

    Add two snowmen (People gallery folder) to a snowy scene. Use a snow template initial world. Then, create a snowman stack by using the scene editor's quad view to position one snowman on top of the other (vertically), as shown below.

3. *Snowpeople Pile*

    Build a "wall" of four snowpeople by tipping them over on their sides and piling them on top of one another. (Use methods, mouse controls, and quad view.) Four snowpeople (alternating between snowman and snowwoman) might be used to produce a wall that looks like this:

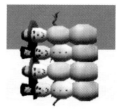

4. *Tea Party*

    As a tribute to Lewis Carroll, create a Tea Party for Alice Liddell and the white rabbit. In addition to AliceLiddell (People) and the whiteRabbit (Animals), the party should include a table (Dining Table in Furniture folder on CD or Web gallery) and three chairs (Furniture), a teapot, a toaster, and a plate (Kitchen). Use method instructions, the mouse, and quad view to properly position objects like the teapot and creamer on the table. The picture below is provided as an example. Use your imagination to make a better scene, if you wish.

5. *Soldiers on Deck (Challenging)*

    Add a carrier (Vehicle) and four toy soldiers (People) to a new world. Line up the soldiers for a formal ceremony—two on each end of the carrier deck, as shown below.

Right-click on each soldier and use methods (from the popup menu) to move the arms of the soldiers to salute each other. Or, use the mouse controls in the scene editor to move the arms into position. (Use the "affect subparts" checkbox to allow the mouse to move their arms.) Raise the left arm of each soldier (at about a 45-degree angle with the horizontal plane). The result should be a scene where all four soldiers are saluting. This is not an animation—all you are trying to do is set up the scene.

**Hint:**   If you check the "affect subparts" checkbox to allow the mouse to move subparts of an object, remember to uncheck the box before using the mouse for some other purpose!

## Summary

At the end of each chapter, we will present a summary and a list of important concepts. The purpose of a summary is to pull together the information and ideas presented in the chapter into a meaningful whole. The purpose of a list of important concepts is to provide a quick review and study guide.

In this chapter, a computer program was presented as a sequence of instructions that tell the computer what to do. Importantly, a computer program is also a way to tell another human being what you want the computer to do. Learning to think about arranging a sequence of instructions to carry out a task (how to design a program) is probably the most important part of learning to program.

Alice is a 3D animation software tool that can be used to learn how to design and write computer programs. Alice allows you to quickly create cartoon-like animations of objects in a 3D virtual world. The objects are three dimensional, having width, height, and depth. Each object has an orientation that provides a sense of direction. That is, an object "knows" which way is up, down, left, right, forward, and backward relative to itself.

### Important concepts in this chapter

- A computer program is a sequence of instructions that tell the computer what to do. It is also a sequence of instructions that tells another human being what you want the computer to do.
- Learning to program is actually learning how to think about arranging a sequence of instructions to carry out a task.
- In Alice, the animation of 3D objects takes place in a virtual world.
- Alice provides a huge number of 3D models. The 3D models are available on the CD accompanying this textbook, as well as on the Alice website at http://www.alice.org
- An Alice object has six degrees of freedom to move around in a virtual world. We call the six degrees of freedom (possible directions of motion) the object's orientation.
- An Alice object has a unique center set by the graphic artist when the 3D model is first created. The center of the ground in an Alice world is located at the position (0, 0, 0).

# Chapter 2

# Program Design and Implementation

*"Then you should say what you mean,"*
*the March Hare went on.*
*"I do," Alice hastily replied; "at least—at least*
*I mean what I say—that's the same thing,*
*you know."*
*"Not the same thing a bit!" said the Hatter.*
*"You might just as well say that 'I see what*
*I eat' is the same thing as 'I eat what I see'!"*

In this chapter we begin an introduction to programming. A program is a set of instructions that tells the computer what to do. Each instruction is an action to be performed. Writing a program to animate 3D objects in a virtual world is naturally all about objects and the actions objects can perform. From a practical viewpoint, writing a program is somewhat like working with word problems in math. We first read the word problem (a description of the situation) and decide how to go about solving it (what steps need to be done). Then, we solve the problem (write a solution) and test our answer to make sure it is correct. Similarly, in writing an animation program we first read a scenario (a description of the story, game, or simulation—often called the problem statement) and decide how to go about creating the animation (design a storyboard). Then we write the program code (implement) and test it by running the animation.

As in Alice's conversation with the March Hare (see above), you must say exactly what you mean when you write a program. The best way to write a program is to begin by reading a scenario (the description of the story, game, or simulation) and then design a list of actions for the program.

Section 2-1 begins with scenarios and storyboards as a methodology for designing programs. Visual storyboards were chosen because they are the design tool used by professional animators in film studios. Textual storyboards were chosen because they provide an algorithmic (step-by-step) structure. The lines of text in a textual storyboard are similar to pseudocode—a loose version of the instructions that will eventually become program code.

Section 2-2 presents the basics of creating a simple program in Alice. The idea is to use a storyboard as a guide for writing the program (list of instructions) in Alice's mouse-based editor. We can focus on a step-by-step solution because Alice will automatically take care of all the details of syntax (statement structure and punctuation). In an animation, some actions must take place in sequence and others simultaneously. This means the program code must be structured to tell Alice which actions to *Do in order* and which to *Do together*.

## 2-1 Scenarios and storyboards

Creating a computer program that animates objects in a virtual world is a four-step process: read the scenario (a description of the problem or task), design (plan ahead), implement (write the program), and test (see if it works). This section introduces the first two steps.

Reading the scenario and designing a plan of action are important steps in constructing programs for animation. A design is a "plan ahead" strategy and takes practice to master. While the programs presented in the first few chapters of this text are reasonably clear-cut, we think it is advisable to start building good designs early on. Then, when programs begin to get more complicated, the time invested in learning how to design good program solutions will pay great dividends.

## Read the scenario

Before we can discuss how to create a design, we need to know what problem is going to be solved or what task is going to be performed. A scenario is a problem (or task) statement that describes the overall animation in terms of what problem is to be solved or what lesson is to be taught. (Many computer scientists use the term requirements specification. In Alice, the term scenario is easier to relate to the world scene, objects, and actions.) Cartoons and feature-length animated films begin with a scenario created by professional writers, sometimes called the "story." As used here, in addition to the traditional meaning, a story can be a lesson to teach, a game to play, or a simulation.

In an Alice world, a scenario gives all necessary details for setting up the initial scene and then planning a sequence of instructions for the animation. That is, a scenario provides answers to the following questions:

1. What story is to be told?
2. What objects are needed? Some objects will play leading roles in the story while other objects will be used to provide background scenery.
3. What actions are to take place? The actions in the story will eventually become the instructions in the program.

## Scenario example

Let's consider an example scenario: After traveling through space, a robot-manned craft has just made a breathless landing on the surface of a moon. The robot has already climbed out of the lunar Lander and has set up a camera so earthbound scientists at the NASA center in Houston can view this historic event. Through the camera (the scene in our world), we can see the robot, the lunar Lander and some nearby rock formations. Suddenly an alien peeks out from behind a rock and looks at the robot. The robot is surprised and rotates its head all the way around. The robot walks over to take a closer look and the alien hides behind the rocks. Finally, the robot looks at the camera, signals danger, and says "Houston, we have a problem!"

From this scenario, we have answers to questions:

- What story is to be told? This scenario tells a humorous story about a robot's first encounter with an alien on a distant moon.
- What objects are to be used? The objects are the robot, a lunar Lander, and an alien. The background scenery should depict a moon surface in a space world.
- What actions are to take place? The actions include the alien peeking out from behind a rock, the robot turning its head around and moving toward the alien, the alien hiding behind the rocks, and the robot sending a message back to earth.

## Design

A storyboard is the design approach we will use to create a solution to a problem or plan a list of actions to perform a task, as specified in the scenario. At Pixar, Disney, and other major animation studios, animators break down a long scenario into sequences of many short scenarios. For each scenario, a storyboard is created to depict the sequence of scenes. The storyboard may consist of dozens of scene sketches, drawn by animation artists or generated by computer animation specialists using computer software. Figure 2-1-1 illustrates storyboard sketches

**Figure 2-1-1.** Storyboard sketches from *Geri's Game*, courtesy of Pixar®

from *Geri's Game*, an animated short film by Pixar® written and directed by Jan Pinkava. The film won an Oscar for Best Animated Short Film. In this film, the title character plays a game of chess against himself.

The storyboard approach to design that breaks a problem or task down into smaller subproblems or tasks is not unique to computer programmers and animators. Playwrights, for example, break their plays down into individual acts and the acts into individual scenes! Engineers break down complicated systems (e.g., jet airplanes and claw hammers) or devices (e.g., microcircuits) into component parts to make the problem more manageable.

## Visual storyboards

A visual storyboard breaks down a scenario into a sequence of major scenes with transitions between scenes. Each sketch is a representation or a snapshot of a scene (state) in the animation. Each snapshot is associated with objects in certain positions, colors, sizes, and poses. When one or more transitions (changes) occur in the animation, the transition leads to the next scene (state).

The snapshots are numbered in sequence and labeled with necessary information. For short animations, the breakdown might be presented on one large sheet of paper. For more complex designs, a separate sheet of drawing paper might used for each scene, allowing the animation artist to easily rearrange or discard scenes without starting over.

To create a visual storyboard we borrow a technique from professional animators—a sequence of hand-drawn scenes. A visual storyboard template is shown in Figure 2-1-2. Each snapshot is labeled with a Scene Number and contains a sketch or picture showing where the objects are in the scene. The description tells what action is occurring. If sound is appropriate in the animation, the description will include a list of sounds that will be played during the scene. If a comic-book style is desired, text may be included to show the words or phrases that will be displayed in a text bubble. Sound and/or text are used only if needed.

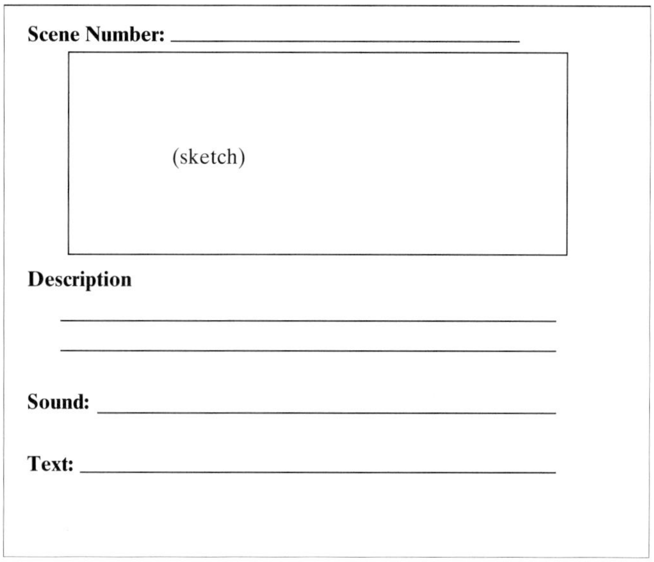

**Scene Number:** _____

(sketch)

**Description**

_____
_____

**Sound:** _____

**Text:** _____

**Figure 2-1-2.** Storyboard template

For our purposes, preparing storyboard sketches is not intended to be a highly artistic task. Simple circles, squares, and lines can be used to represent the objects that will appear in the scene. If necessary, shapes can be labeled with the name of the object or color coded.

To illustrate the creation of a storyboard, the sample scenario for the robot's first encounter will be used. Figure 2-1-3 shows a simple scene where the alien peeks up from behind

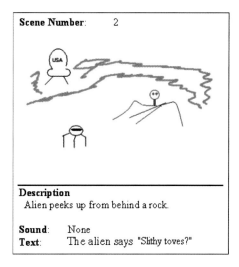

**Scene Number:**   2

**Description**
Alien peeks up from behind a rock.

**Sound:**   None
**Text:**   The alien says "Slithy toves?"

**Figure 2-1-3.** Hand-sketched visual storyboard

a rock. Simple sketches were used to create the lunar Lander, robot, and alien. Brown lines were drawn to create rocks in front of the alien. The grey squiggly lines represent the surface of the moon. Using simple figures, hand-sketched storyboards are quick and easy to create.

For illustrations in this book, we use Alice's scene editor to add objects to a world and then patiently arrange the objects in various poses. As each successive scene is created, a screen capture is made and copied to a document. Figure 2-1-4 illustrates screen captures in a storyboard for the beginning of the robot's first encounter animation. (We used the spiderRobot and the alienOnWheels from the SciFi folder in the gallery.) Naturally, screen captures for a storyboard are fancier than hand-drawn sketches, but they take longer to put together.

Scene Number: 1

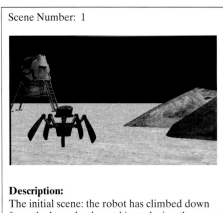

**Description:**
The initial scene: the robot has climbed down from the lunar lander and is exploring the moon surface.

**Sound:** None
**Text:** None

Scene Number: 2

**Description:**
An alien peeks up from behind a rock.

**Sound:** None
**Text:** The alien says "Slithy toves?"

Scene Number: 3

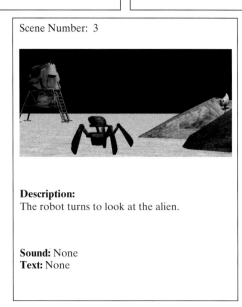

**Description:**
The robot turns to look at the alien.

**Sound:** None
**Text:** None

**Figure 2-1-4.** Screen captures of storyboard scenes

## Textual storyboards

While professional animation artists use visual storyboards as part of their project development process, not everyone has the patience to make dozens of sketches. A textual storyboard is a good alternative. It looks something like a "to-do list" and allows us to prepare a planned structure for writing program code. To take advantage of the strengths of each, both visual and textual storyboards are used throughout this book.

## Textual storyboard example

A textual storyboard for the first encounter animation is shown next. Notice that a textual storyboard may summarize several scenes from a visual storyboard. For instance, the textual storyboard shown here summarizes scene number 1, scene number 2, and scene number 3 from the visual storyboard in Figure 2-1-4. This storyboard represents only the first few actions. It will be completed in the next section.

```
Do the following steps in order
  alien moves up
  alien says "Slithy toves?"
  robot's head turns around
  robot turns to look at alien
Do the following steps together
  robot moves toward the alien
  robot legs walk
etc.
```

The lines of text in a textual storyboard provide an ordered list of actions. The lines are written in an outline format and indentation makes the storyboard easy to read. Notice that two lines are in italics. These lines organize the actions—some actions are to be done in order (one at a time), others are to be done together (at the same time). The first four actions are performed in order (the alien moves up, alien says "Slithy toves?", robot's head turns around, robot turns to look at the alien). The next action, where the robot moves toward the alien to take a closer look, is actually a composite of actions performed simultaneously (the robot moves forward at the same time as the robot's legs simulate a walking action).

In computing terminology, a textual storyboard is called an algorithm—a list of actions to perform a task or solve a problem. The actions in a textual storyboard are very close to (but not quite) actual program code and so they are often known as pseudocode.

## Evaluate and revise

Once a storyboard has been designed, it is a good idea to take an objective look to decide what might be changed. Evaluate the storyboard by answering these questions:

- Does the action flow from scene to scene, as the story unfolds?
- Do any transitions need to be added to blend one scene to the next?
- Did you overlook some essential part of the story?
- Is there something about the story that should be changed?

The important idea is that the storyboard is not final. We should be willing to review our plans and modify them, if necessary. In creating a program design, we go through the same kinds of cycles as an artist who has an idea to paint on a canvas. The painter often sketches a preliminary version of what the painting will look like. This is a way of translating the abstract idea into a more concrete vision. Then, the painter looks at the preliminary version and may change it several times before actually applying oils to the canvas. Likewise, an engineer who designs a bridge or an airplane (or anything else) goes through many design-modify-create phases before the final product is constructed. All creative people go through these design-modify-create cycles.

## 2-2  A first program

In Section 2-1, you learned how to carefully read a scenario and design an animation to carry out a task, play a game, or create a simulation. Now you are ready to look at how an animation program can be written. This step is called implementation. We recommend that you read this section while sitting at a computer: start up Alice and repeat the steps shown in the example in this section.

### What is a program?

As you know, a program is a list of instructions (actions) to accomplish a task. You can think of an Alice program as being somewhat like a script for a theatrical play. A theatrical script tells a story by describing the actions to be taken and the words to be delivered by actors on stage. In a similar manner, an Alice program prescribes the actions to be taken and the sound and text to be used by objects in a virtual world.

### Create an initial scene

An ancient Chinese proverb advises that "The longest journey begins with a single step." Let's begin our journey by implementing the robot first encounter animation described in Section 2-1. Recall that a robot-manned spacecraft has just landed on a moon. The robot encounters an alien that curiously peeks out from behind the rocks. The surprised robot walks toward the alien to check it out and then sends a message back to earth: "Houston, we have a problem!"

The first step in implementing the animation program is to create the initial scene. A space template is selected and then a spiderRobot, alienOnWheels, and lunarLander (from the SciFi folder in the gallery) are added to the world. Rocks (from the Nature folder on the CD or Web gallery) are added and positioned in front of the alien to hide the alien from view. The initial scene is shown in Figure 2-2-1.

**Figure 2-2-1.** First encounter initial scene

### Worlds on the CD

The CD accompanying this book contains the worlds for all examples in the chapters. The worlds have all the objects for the world, properly positioned in the initial scene. The CD worlds do not have the program code—the code is provided in the narrative of each chapter section. We recommend that you sit at a computer, load the CD world for the example and re-construct the program as you read the chapter. This experience will help you learn how to write programs and will also help you get started in creating your own animations.

## Program code editor

Once the initial scene has been set up, the instructions that make up the program code must be written. Alice provides a program code editor—the large yellow pane at the lower right of the main Alice window, as shown in Figure 2-2-2. The instructions for a program are entered in the editor. (From now on, we refer to the program code editor as "the editor.")

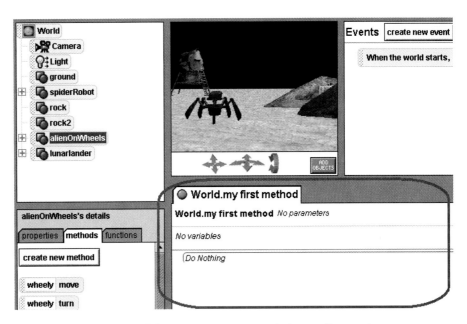

**Figure 2-2-2.** Program code editor (the large yellow pane)

## World.my first method

As seen in Figure 2-2-2, the tab for the editing area is labeled *World.my first method*. A method is a segment of program code (a small set of instructions) that defines how to perform a specific task. Alice automatically uses the name *World.my first method* for the first editing pane. Actually, any name can be made up and used for a method name. We will use the name *World.my first method* for this example. The robot world scenario is simple enough to be programmed in just one method, *World.my first method*. When the **Play** button is pressed, Alice will execute *World.my first method* by carrying out the instructions that we write there.

## What instructions are needed?

Let's take another look at the storyboard presented earlier.

```
Do the following steps in order
  alien moves up
  alien says "Slithy toves?"
  robot's head turns around
  robot turns to look at alien
  Do the following steps together
    robot moves toward the alien
    robot legs walk
  etc.
```

Actually, this storyboard is incomplete because (in the interests of space) we did not finish the story. The scenario described a sequence of actions: (a) the alienOnWheels moves up from behind the rocks, (b) the alienOnWheels says "Slithy toves?", (c) the spiderRobot's head turns around, (d) the spiderRobot turns to look at the alienOnWheels, (e) the spiderRobot moves toward the alienOnWheels to get a closer look, (f) the alienOnWheels hides behind a rock, (g) the spiderRobot looks at the camera, and (h) the spiderRobot says "Houston, we have a problem!" Let's complete the textual storyboard by adding the remaining actions, as shown next.

```
Do the following steps in order
  alien moves up
  alien says "Slithy toves?"
  robot's head turns around
  robot turns to look at alien
  Do together
    robot moves toward the alien
    robot legs walk
  alien moves down
  robot turns to look at the camera
  robot's head turns red (to signal danger)
  robot says "Houston, we have a problem!"
```

## Translating a storyboard to program code

To translate a storyboard to program code, begin with the first step of the storyboard and translate it to an instruction. Then translate the second step to an instruction, then the third, and so forth until the entire storyboard has been translated to instructions. The instructions used in program code are the same built-in methods you learned in the Getting Started exercises in Appendix A. To display the alienOnWheels' available methods, first click the alienOnWheels object in the Object tree and then click the methods tab in the details area, as seen in Figure 2-2-3.

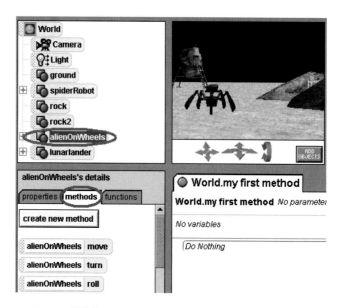

**Figure 2-2-3.** Built-in methods for writing program code

In our example, we want to translate the storyboard to program code. We begin with the first step, making the alienOnWheels peek up from behind the rocks. One of the alienOn-Wheels' methods is *move*—we can use this method to make the alienOnWheels move upward. The next step is to have the alienOnWheels say, "Slithy toves?" The alienOnWheels has a *say* method that can be used for this purpose. In a similar manner, each action in the storyboard will be translated to instructions, using the built-in methods of the objects in the world.

### Sequential versus simultaneous actions

From our storyboard, it is clear that the first four actions must occur one after another, in sequence. We can tell Alice to *Do* these instructions *in order*. Other actions occur simultaneously. For example, the spiderRobot moves forward at the same time as the spiderRobot's legs walk. Alice must be told to *Do* these actions *together*. *Do in order* and *Do together* are part of the Alice language. We call them control statements, because we use them to tell Alice how to carry out the instructions in a program.

### Do in order

To tell Alice to do instructions in sequential order, a *Do in order* block is dragged into the editor, as shown in Figure 2-2-4.

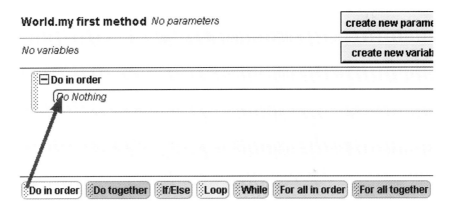

**Figure 2-2-4.** Dragging a *Do in order* tile into the editor

The first four instructions can now be placed within the *Do in order* block. First, the alienOnWheels is selected in the Object tree. Then, the alienOnWheels's *move* method tile is selected and dragged into the *Do in order*, as shown in Figure 2-2-5. The *move* method requires arguments—which *direction* and how far (*distance*) the alienOnWheels should move. (An argument is an item of information that must be supplied so Alice can execute the action.) In this example, the alienOnWheels is hidden behind the rocks and we want the alienOnWheels to move upward so the direction is *up*. The rocks are not very tall, so we will try a distance of 1 meter. (If this distance is not enough or is too much, we can adjust it later.) The method name and its arguments are the components of an instruction.

The resulting instruction is shown in Figure 2-2-6.

The second instruction is to have the alienOnWheels say, "Slithy toves?" Select alienOn-Wheels in the Object tree and drag in the *say* method tile. Select *other* as the argument, as shown in Figure 2-2-7. A popup dialog box provides a text area where you can enter the words you want to appear. Type "Slithy toves?" without the quotes, as illustrated in Figure 2-2-8 and then click OK.

The first two instructions are shown in Figure 2-2-9. When this program is run (it is perfectly fine to try out the effect of just one or two Alice instructions by clicking on the **Play** button), the alienOnWheels will move up from behind the rocks and then say, "Slithy toves?"

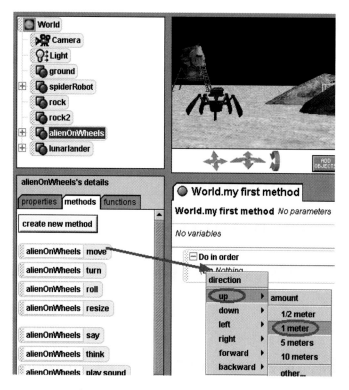

**Figure 2-2-5.** Adding a *move* instruction

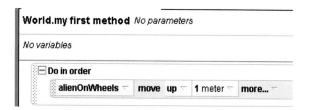

**Figure 2-2-6.** The completed *move* instruction

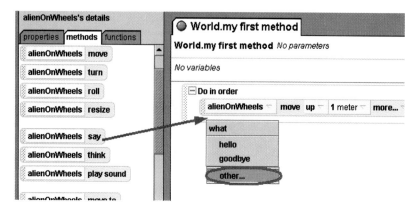

**Figure 2-2-7.** Adding a *say* instruction for alienOnWheels

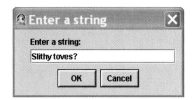

**Figure 2-2-8.** Entering a string

**World.my first method** *No parameters*

*No variables*

```
Do in order
   alienOnWheels   move  up   1 meter   more...
   alienOnWheels   say  Slithy toves?   more...
```

**Figure 2-2-9.** First two instructions

For the third instruction, the spiderRobot's head is to turn around a full revolution (to express surprise). How can we turn the spiderRobot's head? Clicking the + next to spiderRobot in the Object tree causes its subparts to be displayed. Click on the + next to spider Robot's neck in the Object tree. Then clicking on the spiderRobot's head in the Object tree allows access to instructions for moving its head. Drag the *turn* method tile into the editor and select *left* as the direction and *1 revolution* as the amount of turn, as shown in Figure 2-2-10.

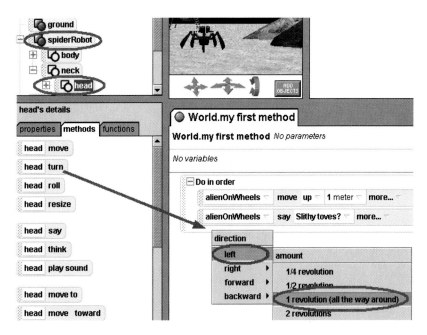

**Figure 2-2-10.** Adding a *turn* instruction for *spiderRobot head*

In the fourth instruction, the spiderRobot will *turn to face* the alienOnWheels. The spiderRobot *turn to face* method tile is dragged into the editor and alienOnWheels is selected as the target argument, as illustrated in Figure 2-2-11.

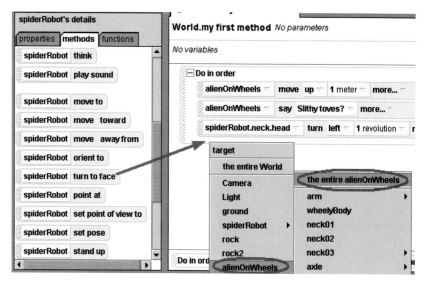

**Figure 2-2-11.** Adding a *turn to face* instruction

The program code with the first four instructions completed is shown in Figure 2-2-12.

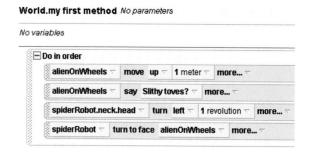

**Figure 2-2-12.** *Do in order* with first four instructions

## Do together

The next step in the storyboard requires two things to occur at once: the spiderRobot moving forward at the same time as its legs move up and down. A *Do together* tile is dragged into the *Do in order*, as shown in Figure 2-2-13. Notice the horizontal (green in the editor) line in Figure 2-2-13. A green line indicates where the *Do together* instruction will be dropped.

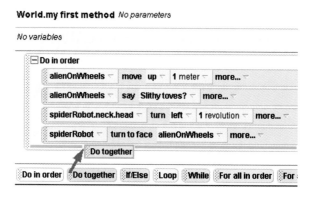

**Figure 2-2-13.** Adding a *Do together* (inside the *Do in order*)

The result of this modification, illustrated in Figure 2-2-14, is that the *Do together* block is nested within the *Do in order* block. Nesting means that one program statement is written inside another. Note that nesting the *Do together* inside the *Do in order* just happens to be the best way to animate this example. A *Do together* does not have to be inside a *Do in order*. These two coding blocks can work together or can work separately in many different combinations.

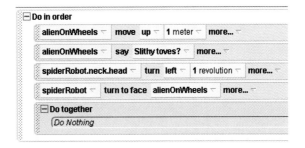

**Figure 2-2-14**. *Do together* nested within a *Do in order*

Now, methods can be dragged into the *Do together* block to simultaneously have the spiderRobot move forward and walk. The *move* forward instruction is easy. Just add a spider-Robot *move* instruction with forward as the *direction* and 1 meter as the *distance*, as illustrated in Figure 2-2-15.

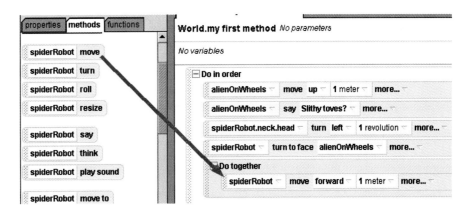

**Figure 2-2-15.** Adding a *move* instruction inside the *Do together*

The spiderRobot has several legs. To simplify our program, we will animate the walking action of just two legs (backLeft and frontRight). A leg walks by turning at a joint (similar to bending your knee). Let's begin by creating an instruction to turn the backLeftLegUpper-Joint. First select the backLeftLegUpperJoint subpart of the backLeftLegBase subpart of the spiderRobot in the Object tree and then drag the *turn* method tile into the *Do together* block, as shown in Figure 2-2-16.

Note that popup menus allow you to select arguments for the *direction* and the *amount* of turn. Select *forward* as the direction and *other* as the amount. When *other* is selected as the amount, a number pad (looks like a calculator) pops up on the screen. We chose 0.1 revolutions, clicking the buttons on the number pad to make our selection. How did we know to use *0.1* revolutions as the amount? Well, we didn't. We just tried several different amounts until we finally found one that worked to give the best bending motion for the leg joint. This is an

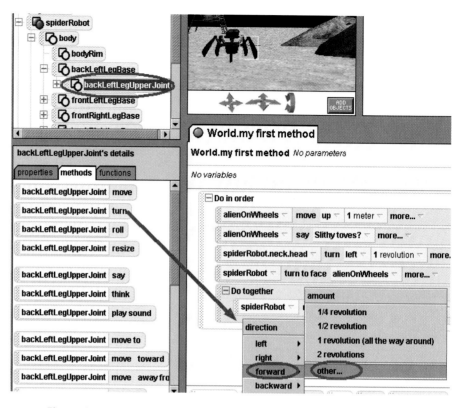

**Figure 2-2-16.** Dragging in a *turn* instruction for the backLeftLegUpperJoint

example of a trial-and-error strategy. While we always recommend good planning strategies, sometimes trial and error is useful.

Naturally, when a leg joint is turned in one direction it must turn back again (to maintain balance). The two *turn* instructions for the backLeft leg are shown in Figure 2-2-17.

```
spiderRobot.body.backLeftLegBase.backLeftLegUpperJoint   turn  forward   0.1 revolutions
spiderRobot.body.backLeftLegBase.backLeftLegUpperJoint   turn  backward  0.1 revolutions
```

**Figure 2-2-17.** Instructions to *turn forward* and *backward*

Using the same technique, instructions are created to turn the frontRight leg. The completed walking instructions are shown in Figure 2-2-18.

**Figure 2-2-18.** Instructions to simulate a walking motion for the spiderRobot

## Bugs

You will recall that the four steps in creating an animation program are: read, design, implement, and test. Now that several lines of code have been written (implemented), it is a good idea to test whether what you have written thus far works the way you thought it would. You do not have to wait until the entire program is completed. To test the instructions written thus far, the **Play** button is clicked. The alienOnWheels pops up from behind the rocks and then says "Slithy toves?" The spiderRobot's head turns around and then the spiderRobot turns to face the alienOnWheels. So far so good, but when the spiderRobot moves forward, the legs do not walk. That is, the leg joints do not appear to turn at all!

The reason the leg joints do not turn is that the program has a bug. (Errors in computer programs are generally referred to as bugs. When we remove bugs from a program, we debug the program.) The problem is, in the code shown above, the leg joint *turn* instructions are written inside a *Do together*. Of course, if the joints turn both forward and backward at the same time, they effectively cancel each other and the spiderRobot's legs do not walk at all! To fix this problem, it is necessary to place the backLeft leg-joint-turn instructions within a *Do in order* block and also the frontRight leg-joint-turn instructions within a *Do in order* block, as illustrated in Figure 2-2-19.

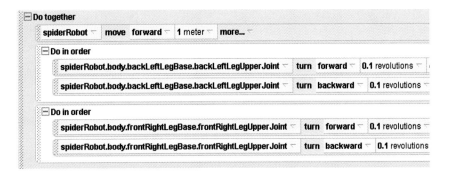

**Figure 2-2-19.** Revised instructions for walking the spiderRobot's legs

Now the spiderRobot's backLeft and frontRight legs walk! There is one other useful observation to make. Animation instructions, by default, require one second to run. Normally, within a *Do together* block, each of the instructions should take the same amount of time. Since it takes one second for the spiderRobot to move forward 1 meter, the walking action of each leg should also take one second. However, there are two steps in bending the leg joint (forward and then backward). Each step in bending the leg joint should require one-half second. To change the duration, click on *more ...* (at the far right of the instruction where the duration is to be changed), select the *duration* menu item, and select *0.5 seconds*, as shown in Figure 2-2-20.

**Figure 2-2-20.** Changing the *duration* of an instruction

## Using a property

We still need to complete the final four actions described in the storyboard (alienOnWheels moves down, the spiderRobot turns to face the camera, spiderRobot's head turns red, and spiderRobot says "Houston, we have a problem!"). You have already used a *move, turn to face,* and *say* instruction—so these will be easy to create. The only new instruction is the one that requires the spiderRobot's head to turn red (a danger signal). To make this happen, we use the color property of the spiderRobot's head. To view the list of properties of the spiderRobot's head, select the spiderRobot's head in the Object tree and select the properties tab in the details area (lower left of the Alice window), as shown in Figure 2-2-21.

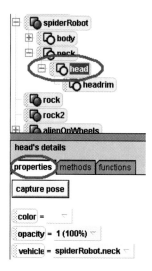

**Figure 2-2-21.** The properties of the spiderRobot's head

What we want to do is change the color of the spiderRobot's head after it turns to face the camera. Of course, the properties can be changed when the initial world is created. But, we want to change the color property while the animation is running. (The technical term for "while the animation is running" is "at runtime.") An instruction must be created to set the color. Figure 2-2-22 demonstrates dragging in the color property tile to create a set instruction. The color tile in the properties list for the spiderRobot's head is dragged into the *Do in order* block. Then, the *color* red is selected from the popup menu of available colors.

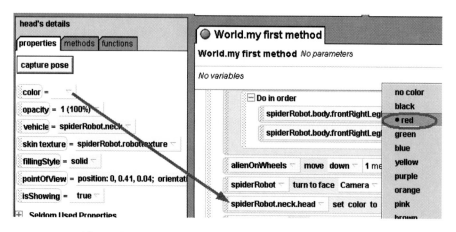

**Figure 2-2-22.** Changing the *color* of the spiderRobot's head

The final code for the entire animation is listed in Figure 2-2-23.

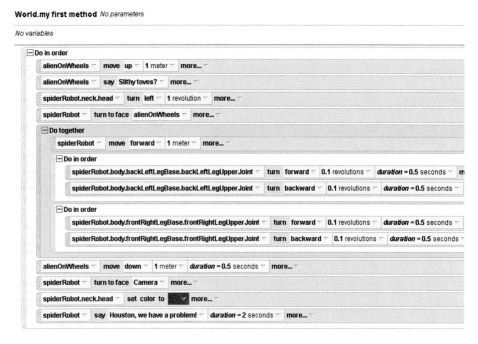

**Figure 2-2-23.**  The program code for the entire first encounter animation

## Comments

Now that we have written our first program, it is time to look at a useful component in programs—comments. Comments are NOT instructions that cause some action to take place. This means that Alice can ignore comments when running a program. However, comments are considered good programming "style" and are extremely useful for humans who are reading a program. Comments help the human reader understand what a program does. This is particularly helpful when someone else wants to read your program code to see what you wrote and how you wrote it.

Comments in Alice are created by dragging the green // tile into a program and then writing a description of what a sequence of code is intended to do. Figure 2-2-24 illustrates *World.my first method* with a comment added. Where it is not obvious, a comment should be included at the beginning of a method to explain what the method does. This kind of comment is like writing a topic sentence in a paragraph—it summarizes what is going on.

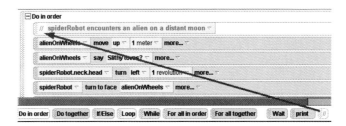

**Figure 2-2-24.**  An overview comment for *World.my first method*

Also, small sections of several lines of code that collectively perform some action can be documented using a comment. An additional comment has been added in Figure 2-2-25.

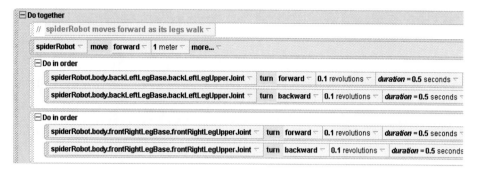

**Figure 2-2-25.** A comment for a small section of code

This comment explains that this small section of the code is to have the spiderRobot move forward as its legs walk.

## Tips & Techniques 2
## Orientation and Movement Instructions

### The *orient to* method

Each object in an Alice world has its own coordinate system that provides a sense of direction—its orientation. To illustrate the way the coordinate system provides orientation for an object, we implanted a visible set of axes (Shapes) into the monkey (Animals) shown in Figure T-2-1.

**Figure T-2-1.** The monkey's orientation

When two objects must move together, the orientation of the two objects must be synchronized. In the world shown in Figure T-2-2, we want the monkey to stay on top of toyball (Sports) as the ball moves forward for a short distance.

The code we wrote to make the monkey and ball move forward together is shown in Figure T-2-3.

Imagine our surprise when the ball moved in one direction and the monkey moved in a different direction, ending up well away from the ball, suspended in midair. Why did this happen? Well, the ball is an example of an object for which we can't tell (just by looking at it) which direction is forward and which direction is backward. Evidently, in positioning the ball and the monkey in the scene, we positioned the ball so its forward direction was not the same as the forward direction for the monkey, as illustrated in Figure T-2-4. So, when the ball and the monkey each move forward, they move in different directions.

**Figure T-2-2.**  The monkey jumps on top of a toyball

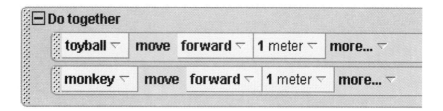

**Figure T-2-3.**  Code to move toyball and monkey forward together

**Figure T-2-4.**  The monkey and toyball move forward in different directions

The way to solve this problem is to synchronize the orientation of the two objects. In this example, we will use a *toyball.orient to(monkey)* instruction, as shown in Figure T-2-5.

The result is shown in Figure T-2-6. Now, the toy ball has the same orientation (the same sense of direction) as the monkey. This means that the two objects will move in the same direction when a *move forward* instruction is given to each.

The *orient to* instruction may seem a bit weird, but it simply tells Alice that the first object should take on the same sense of direction as the second object. So, if we orient two objects to

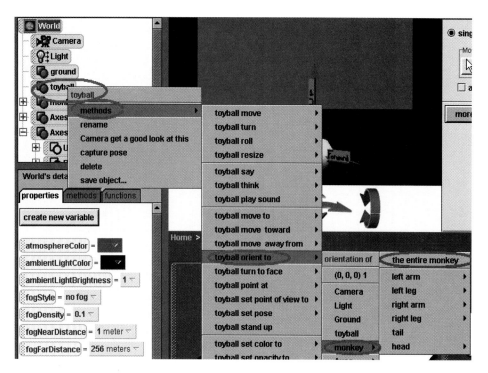

**Figure T-2-5.** Cascading menus for *orient to*

**Figure T-2-6.** Now the monkey and the toyball have the same orientation

have the same orientation, then the two objects are synchronized—they have the same sense of up, down, left, right, forward, and backward.

### The *vehicle* property

Another way to synchronize the movements of two objects is to take advantage of a special property called *vehicle*. As an illustration of the vehicle property, consider a circus act where a chicken (Animals) rides on the back of a horse (Animals), as seen in Figure T-2-7. As part of the circus act, the horse trots around in a circular path and the chicken rides on the back of the horse.

To synchronize the movement of the chicken and the horse, you can make the horse be a *vehicle* for the chicken. To create this special effect, select chicken in the object tree and then

**Figure T-2-7.**  Circus act, chicken riding on horse

select the properties tab (under the object tree at the lower left of the window). Then click on the white tile to the right of the word vehicle. A list of possible vehicles is shown in a popup menu, from which horse can be selected, as illustrated in Figure T-2-8. Now, when the horse moves, the chicken will move with it.

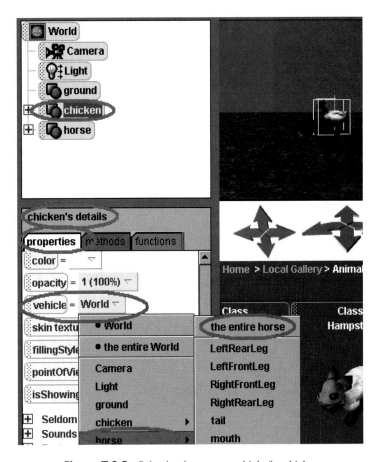

**Figure T-2-8.**  Selecting horse as a vehicle for chicken

## Arguments: *duration, style, asSeenBy*

Movement instructions (e.g., *move, turn, roll*) end with the editing tag "*more...*", as in Figure T-2-9.

**Figure T-2-9.** The *more . . .* editing tag

When *more . . .* is clicked, a popup menu allows you to select from a list of three arguments, *duration, style,* and *asSeenBy*—as shown in Figure T-2-10.

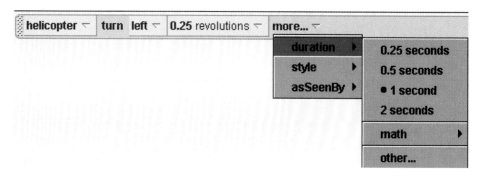

**Figure T-2-10.** Popup menu for *more . . .*

The *duration* argument tells Alice an amount of time (in seconds) for animating the movement. (Alice assumes that the amount of time for a movement is 1 second.) A zero (0) duration is an instantaneous movement. Negative values are not used. In the First Encounter example in this chapter, a *duration* argument was used to shorten the amount of time for turning the robot's leg joints to simulate walking.

The *style* argument specifies the way in which one movement instruction blends into the next. The options are *gently* (begin and end gently), *abruptly* (begin and end abruptly), *begin gently* (and end abruptly), and *end gently* (and begin abruptly). To get the right degree of "smoothness" for a movement, it is often worthwhile to experiment with *style*.

As described in Chapter 1, each object in Alice has its own sense of direction (orientation). But, you can use the *asSeenBy* argument to tell Alice to use an orientation of one object to guide the movement of another object. This is best explained by using an example. Suppose we have a helicopter (Vehicles in CD or Web gallery) on a pilot training mission, as shown in Figure T-2-11.

**Figure T-2-11.** Training mission

The code in Figure T-2-12 is intended to roll the helicopter left and then move it upward.

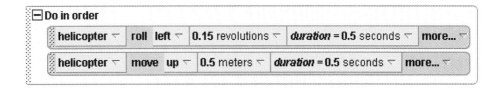

**Figure T-2-12.** Code to *roll* and then *move* upward

Running the animation, we see that the result is not what we had in mind. When the helicopter moves upward, it does so from its own sense of direction, as in Figure T-2-13.

**Figure T-2-13.** Up—from the helicopter's sense of direction (orientation)

What we had wanted, however, was an upward movement with respect to the ground. To correct this problem, we clicked on *more . . .* and then selected *asSeenBy* → *ground*, as in Figure T-2-14.

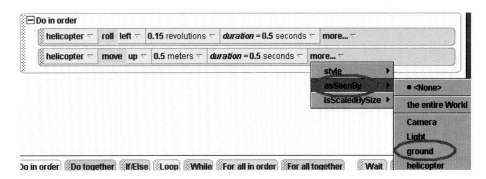

**Figure T-2-14.** Selecting *asSeenBy* Ground

The resulting code, shown in Figure T-2-15, gives the desired movement.

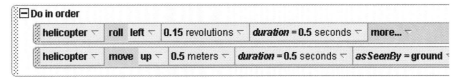

**Figure T-2-15.** The modified code

## The *turn to face* and *point at* methods

As discussed above, the *asSeenBy* argument in a movement instruction uses the orientation of one object to guide the movement of another object. Two special methods are also useful for making an object turn to "look at" another object. A *turn to face* method causes one object to pivot around until its front is facing some other object. In the previous section of this chapter, *turn to face* was used to have the spiderRobot turn to look at the alienOnWheels.

A second method, *point at*, can be used to align two objects from the center of one to the center of another. It is easiest to explain *point at* in an example. In Figure T-2-16, the rowers in the lifeboat (Vehicles) want to row toward the lighthouse (Beach) on the island (Environments). An obvious first step is to have the boat and the rowers turn to look at the lighthouse on the island.

**Figure T-2-16.** The lighthouse, island, and boat initial scene

The *point at* method may be used to aim the boat at the lighthouse location. Then, movement instructions may be used to move the boat toward the island and the lighthouse, as in Figure T-2-17.

**Figure T-2-17.** Code to aim the boat toward the lightHouse

While this instruction does turn the lifeboat toward the lighthouse, it also has the effect of tipping the boat so it seems to be sinking on one end, as seen in Figure T-2-18.

**Figure T-2-18.** The lifeboat tips on the *point at* instruction

The *point at* instruction aligns the center of the lifeboat with the center of the lighthouse, which is higher in elevation than the boat, as shown in Figure T-2-19. As a result, the boat tips.

**Figure T-2-19.**  Alignment from center to center

You may, or may not, want the boat to tip. To provide some control of the *point at* instruction, additional arguments are available in the *more ...* popup menu, as seen in Figure T-2-20. Selecting *true* for the *onlyAffectYaw* argument allows an object to point at another object without tipping (pitching). Yaw is a technical term meaning a left-right turning motion, and pitch is a tipping, rocking-chair kind of motion. (When *onlyAffectYaw* is *true,* the *point at* instruction works the same as a *turn to face* instruction.) Note that in target games and flight animations *onlyAffectYaw* should be *false* (so as to align on the diagonal with a target object).

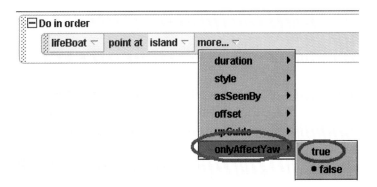

**Figure T-2-20.**  Selecting *onlyAffectYaw* $\rightarrow$ *true*

## Exercises

### 2-1 Exercises

1. *Creating Storyboards*
   Create a visual and a textual storyboard (two storyboards) for each of the following scenarios:

   (a) A child's game: Alice, the white rabbit, and the Cheshire cat enjoy a game of musical chairs in a tea party scene. One of the characters yells "switch" and they all run around the table to stand beside the next chair. After the switch, a chair is tipped over and the character standing next to it is eliminated from the game (moves away from the table).

(b) A video game: A jet fighter plane is returning to the carrier deck after a training mission. The plane makes a half-circle around the carrier to get into position for landing and then gradually descends. The carrier is in motion, so the plane has to continually adjust its descent to finally land on the deck. After the plane touches down on the carrier, it continues to move across the deck to finally come to a halt.

(c) An Olympic simulation: An ice skater is practicing her skating routine for the Olympic trials. She will perform a sequence of jumps and spins, while classical music is playing.

## 2-2 Exercises

2. *First Encounter—Extended*

(a) The worlds used for chapter examples throughout this book can be found on the CD. Each world provided on the CD has the initial scene already set up with the background scenery and the objects, as shown in the example. In this chapter, the example world is a first encounter, where a robot meets an alien on a distant moon. Start Alice. Then, copy the *FirstEncounter.a2w* world to your computer. In Alice, use **File|Open** to open the world. Follow along with the reading in the chapter and recreate the program as described in the chapter.

(b) In the code presented in this chapter, only two legs (backLeft and frontRight) were animated in a walking action. Add code to animate a walking action for the other legs. Be sure to save the world.

3. *Snowpeople*

Create a snow people world as shown in the scene below. Several snow people are outdoors on a snow-covered landscape.

A snowman is trying to meet a snowwoman who is talking with a friend (another snowwoman.) The snowman tries to get her attention. He turns to face the snowwoman and says "Ahem." She turns to look at the snowman and he blinks his eyes at her. She blushes (her head turns red). But, alas, she is not interested in meeting him. She gives him a "cold shoulder" and turns back to talk with her friend. He hangs his head in disappointment and turns away.

4. *Circling Fish*

Create an island world with a fish in the water. (You may wish to reuse the island world created in an exercise for Chapter 1.) Position the fish and the camera point of view so the scene appears as illustrated below. Write a program that has the fish swim around in a circle in front of the island. Next, have the fish swim around the island. You may wish to have the fish move *asSeenBy* the island (*asSeenBy* is described in Tips & Techniques 2).

Finally, have the fish jump out of the water and then dive down into the water. The final scene should look somewhat like the initial scene, with the fish back in roughly the same position as where it started.

5. *Tortoise Gets a Cookie*

Create a world having a tortoise (Animals), a stool (Furniture in CD or Web gallery), and a cookie (Kitchen/Food), as shown below. Put the cookie on top of the stool. (Cookies are the tortoise's favorite snack food.) Position the tortoise and the stool side by side and then use a *move* method to move the tortoise 2 meters away from the stool. (This way, you know exactly how far the tortoise is from the stool.) Use a *turn to face* method to be sure the tortoise is facing the stool. Write a program to move the tortoise to the stool to get the cookie. Have the tortoise show its thanks (for the cookie) by looking at the camera and waving an arm.

## Summary

This chapter introduced the fundamental concepts of programming in Alice. We began with reading the scenario and designing a storyboard. A scenario helps us set the stage—that is, it tells us what objects will be used and what actions they will perform. A storyboard breaks down a scenario into a sequence of scenes that provide a sense of the order in which actions will take place.

Some actions in a program will take place in sequence (one after the other) and some actions simultaneously (at the same time). Once prepared, a storyboard is used as a guide for implementation (writing the program code). Testing code (running the program) is an important step in finding and removing bugs (errors in the program).

Comments are used to document methods, where the purpose of the method or a small section of a method is not immediately obvious. Comments are considered good programming "style."

## Important concepts in this chapter

- A scenario is a problem statement that describes the overall animation in terms of what problem is to be solved, what lesson is to be taught, what game played, or what simulation demonstrated.

- A storyboard can be visual or textual.

- A visual storyboard is a sequence of hand-drawn sketches or screen captures that break down a scenario into a sequence of major scenes with transitions between scenes.

- Each sketch represents a state of the animation—sort of a snapshot of the scene—showing the position, color, size, and other properties of objects in the scene.

- A textual storyboard is somewhat like a to-do list, providing an algorithmic list of steps that describe sequential and/or simultaneous actions.

- A program consists of lines of code that specify the actions objects are to perform.

- The characters you see in an Alice world are known as objects. We write program statements to make the objects move by dragging their action instructions (methods) into the editor.

- In Alice, program code is structured in *Do in order* and *Do together* blocks to tell Alice which instructions are to be executed in order and which are to be executed simultaneously.

- Complicated animations may be constructed from simple compositions of *Do in order* and *Do together* blocks of code. Knowing what each means and knowing how to combine them (by nesting one inside the other) is powerful; it provides an easy way to put together more complicated actions.

# Chapter 3

## Programming: Putting Together the Pieces

*"Let me think: was I the same when I got up this morning? I almost think I can remember feeling a little different. But if I'm not the same, the next question is, 'Who in the world am I? Ah, THAT'S the great puzzle!"*

In this chapter, you will see how to put together different kinds of program code "pieces" to make the program do what you want it to do. The pieces of program code will include:

*instruction*—a statement that executes to make objects perform a certain action

*control structure*—a statement that controls the execution of a block of instructions

*function*—asks a question about a condition or computes a value

*expression*—a math operation on numbers or other kinds of values

You have already seen instructions such as:

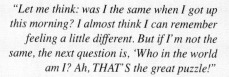

You have also been using the *Do in order* and *Do together* control structures. The *Do in order* structure tells Alice to run the instructions sequentially, one after the other. The *Do together* structure tells Alice to run the instructions all at the same time.

This chapter presents two additional execution controls: conditional execution (*If/Else*) and repetition. This is where programming gets exciting, because you gain control of how the program is executed. Conditional execution makes use of functions and expressions to check a current condition in the world. For example, "Is the color of the spiderRobot's head red?" Obviously, this is a question and a function is used to ask the question. Often, checking a condition requires that two or more objects be compared. For example, we might check whether "the distance of the spiderRobot from a rock is greater than 1 meter." An expression is used to compare whether the distance between the two objects is greater than 1 meter.

Section 3-1 uses short examples to show how to use built-in functions in Alice. We also look at simple arithmetic operations (addition, subtraction, multiplication, and division) in expressions.

Section 3-2 introduces conditional execution in the form of an *If/Else* statement. An *If/Else* statement involves making a decision based on a current condition in the world. A simple repetition control structure is also introduced, in the form of a *Loop* statement. A *Loop* statement repeats the execution of a section of program code a specific number of times.

## **3-1** Built-in functions and expressions

As you know, information about the world and objects within the world is stored in properties. We can use a function to ask questions about these properties. Also, we can perform arithmetic operations on the values of these properties by using expressions. The focus of this section is on how to use properties, functions, and expressions to allow a program to work with information about a world and its objects.

### Built-in functions

Not all properties of objects are available in its properties list. Only properties most commonly used in setting up your world (for example, *color* and *opacity*) are listed. Other properties of objects (such as *height, width,* and *position*) can be determined, however, by asking Alice for the information. The Alice system provides a set of built-in *functions*—statements you can use to ask about properties of objects and relationships of objects to one another. Also, utilitarian kinds of questions can be asked of the world—about things like the position of the mouse and some math operations.

To better understand why we want to use functions, let's look again at the First Encounter world, shown in Figure 3-1-1. As you view this scene, you interpret what you see. For

**Figure 3-1-1.** Initial scene from the First Encounter world

example, you pick up visual clues in the scene that lead you to believe that the spiderRobot is closer to the camera than the rocks. An artist calls this perspective. Of course, it is difficult to know exactly how far away the rocks are from the spiderRobot. Likewise, it is difficult to know how far the spiderRobot is away from the lunarLander. The camera angle simply does not provide enough information.

This is where functions come into play. Functions can be used to get the information we need. Alice provides several functions that can be used for each object in a world. We call these built-in functions. To view a list of built-in functions about an object in a world, select the object in the Object tree and view the functions in the details area. In this example, you can view a list of built-in functions for the spiderRobot by selecting spiderRobot in the Object tree and then its functions tab, as in Figure 3-1-2.

At the right of the functions list, a scroll bar allows you to scroll the window down to view all the available functions for the spiderRobot. The built-in functions are divided into subcategories:

**Proximity**—how close the object is to some other object in the world (such as *distance to, distance above*). (The functions in Figure 3-1-2 are **proximity** functions.)

**Size**—dimensions such as height, width, and depth, and how these compare to the dimensions of another object in the world

**Spatial relation**—orientation compared to another object in the world (such as *to left of, to right of*)

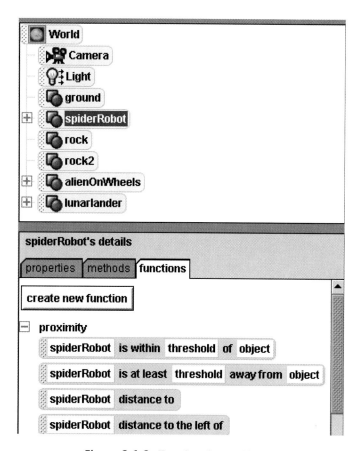

**Figure 3-1-2.** Functions for an object

**Point of view**—position in the world

**Other**—miscellaneous items such as the name of a subpart of the object

In our daily conversations, when a question is asked, we expect to receive an answer. In Alice, the answer is the value of the property you are asking about. What types of values can you expect? That depends on what question the function is asking. For example, the proximity function spiderRobot *is within threshold of object* (*is within threshold* means "is within a given distance") will return a *true* or *false* value. But the function, spiderRobot *distance to*, returns a number (*distance to* means "the distance in meters to another object").

In Alice, values can be of several different types. Four common types of values are:

number (for example, 5 or −19.5)

Boolean value (*true* or *false*)

string (for example, "*hello world*")

object (for example, a *spiderRobot*)

In the first program for the First Encounter world, the spiderRobot wants to get a closer look at the alien. So the spiderRobot moves forward 1 meter as the legs walk. The code is repeated in Figure 3-1-3.

We don't know exactly how far the spiderRobot is away from the rock where the alienOnWheels is hiding. The 1 meter distance for the move forward instruction is just a guess. The problem is that we don't know exactly how far to move the spiderRobot forward. One way to find out is to use trial and error—that is, try different distances until we find one that works best. Another technique to find the distance is to use a function to ask a question: "What is the

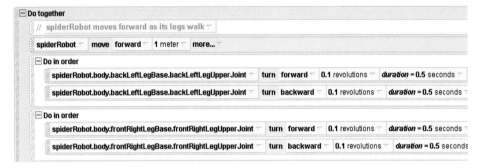

**Figure 3-1-3.** Code to move the spiderRobot forward as the legs walk

spiderRobot's distance to the rock (where the alienOnWheels is hiding)?" Alice will return the distance (in meters). Then the spiderRobot can be moved forward that distance.

To use the *distance to* function, just drag the spiderRobot's *distance to* tile into the editor and drop it on top of the 1 meter distance. Then, select rock as the target object, as shown in Figure 3-1-4.

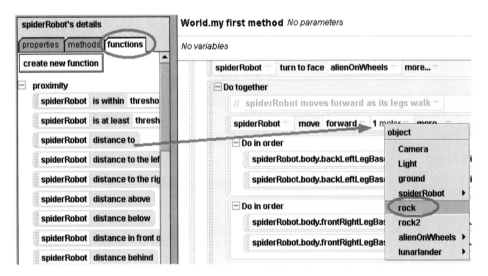

**Figure 3-1-4.** Dragging the *distance to* function into the editor

The resulting code is:

## Collision

After making such a change to our program, the program should be tested. In this example, when the program is run the spiderRobot walks right into the middle of the rock! This is called a collision. In some animations, a collision is exactly what is desired. In this example, though, we do not want the spiderRobot to collide with the rock. The reason a collision occurs is that *distance to* is measured from the center of one object to the center another object. In this example, *distance to* is measured from the spiderRobot's center to the rock's center, as shown in Figure 3-1-5.

**Figure 3-1-5.** The *distance to* function is measured center-to-center

## Expressions

How can a collision be avoided between these two objects? One way is to adjust the distance that the spiderRobot moves so it doesn't move the entire distance. Adjusting the distance requires the use of an arithmetic expression to subtract a small value from the distance. In this example, the rock is bigger than the spiderRobot. If the width of the rock is subtracted from the distance between the two objects, a collision can be avoided.

Alice provides math operators for common math expressions: add $(+)$, subtract $(-)$, multiply $(*)$, and divide $(/)$. A math expression is obtained by selecting *math* from the popup menu of number value in an instruction. For example, to use a math expression to adjust the distance the spiderRobot moves, click the down icon at the far right of the *distance to* tile in the *move* instruction, then select *math* → spiderRobot *distance to* rock $-$ 1, as illustrated in Figure 3-1-6.

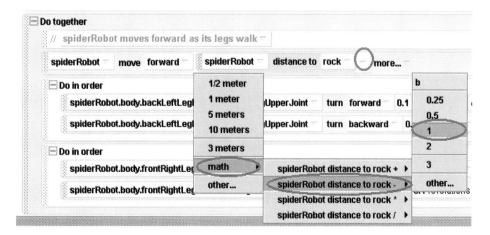

**Figure 3-1-6.** Using a math expression

The resulting instruction subtracts 1 meter from the distance. Actually, we want to subtract the width of the rock from the distance (not 1 meter). But, we had to choose something from the popup menu so we arbitrarily chose 1 meter. This is okay to do because we can now substitute the rock's width for the 1 meter value, as shown in Figure 3-1-7.

**Figure 3-1-7.** Substituting the rock's *width* function for the arbitrary 1 meter value

Now, the spiderRobot moves forward so it gets close to the rock without a collision. The completed code is shown in Figure 3-1-8.

**Figure 3-1-8.** Code to move spiderRobot forward and avoid collision with the rock

*Technical Note:* The distance expression used in the *move* instruction of this example works very well. We should note, however, that this expression is purposely a primitive form of collision detection. To be more technically correct, a collision detection would be computed by subtracting the sum of half the spiderRobot's width and half the rock's width from the total distance (spiderRobot *distance to* rock), as shown in the following code.

## 3-2  Simple control structures

In order to create a program that does more than just execute a few simple instructions, you will need to use control structures. A control structure is a programming statement that allows you to control the order in which instructions are executed. You have already seen two control structures: *Do in order* and *Do together*. This section introduces two more execution control structures: conditional execution and repetition. Conditional execution is where some condition is checked and a decision is made about whether (or not) a certain section of the program code will be executed. Repetition is where a section of the code is run a number of times.

## Conditional execution

A conditional execution control statement depends on a decision. Sometimes life is "one decision after another." If the grass isn't wet, we can mow the lawn. If the dishwasher is full of dirty dishes, we run the dishwasher. If we are taking the dog out for a walk, we put a leash on the dog. Programming, too, often requires *making decisions.* Decisions are useful when writing programs where some instructions are expected to run only under certain conditions.

When a decision is being made, a question is asked about a current condition in the world. For example, "Is the space ship visible?" or "is the color of the hat red?" Clearly the answer is either *true* or *false.* *True* and *false* values are known as Boolean values, named after the 19th century English mathematician, George Boole, who was the first (as far as we know) to be interested in expressions that can evaluate only to either *true* or *false.*

In Alice, an *If/Else* statement is used as a conditional execution control structure. (For convenience, we refer to an *If/Else* statement as an *If* statement.) Figure 3-2-1 illustrates the processing of an *If* statement. The statement checks to see whether a condition is *true.* If the condition is *true,* one set of program instructions is run. If the condition is *false,* a separate set of program instructions is run. The section of code that is executed (or not) depends on the value of the condition.

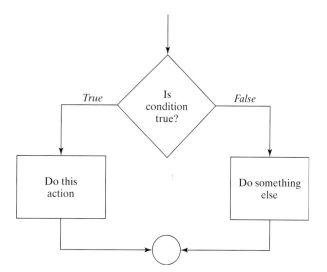

**Figure 3-2-1.** How an *If* statement is processed

An *If* statement is created in Alice by dragging the *If/Else* tile into the editor. A popup box allows you to select the initial condition (*true* or *false*), as shown in Figure 3-2-2.

The green color of this block is a visual clue that an *If* statement is being used in the program. The *If* statement has two parts (an *If* part and an *Else* part). Although an initial condition (*true* or *false*) is selected from the popup menu, Alice allows you to create your own conditional expression on top of the condition tile. A conditional expression is a function that will evaluate (at runtime) to either *true* or *false.* If the answer is *true,* the *If* part is executed and the *Else* part is skipped. But, if the answer is *false,* then the *If* part is skipped and the *Else* part is executed.

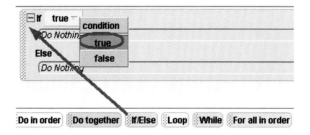

**Figure 3-2-2.** Using an *If* statement

## A simple example

To illustrate the usefulness of an *If* statement, let's continue with First Encounter world. As mentioned before, our sense of perspective can be misleading about distances and sizes of objects in a world. The spiderRobot walks over to the rock to get a closer look at the alienOnWheels, but then the alienOnWheels moves down (out of our sight). From this camera angle, as seen in Figure 3-2-3, the rock appears to be taller than the robot, but we cannot be sure. So we cannot tell whether the spiderRobot is actually able to see over the rock. If the spiderRobot is shorter than the rock, it could move its neck up to look over the rock. Otherwise, the spiderRobot can still see the alienOnWheels and no additional action is necessary.

**Figure 3-2-3.** The spiderRobot moves closer, but the alienOnWheels hides behind the rock

The problem is, how do we know which is taller (the spiderRobot or the rock)? One solution is to use an *If* statement with the built-in *is shorter than* question. The storyboard is:

```
If spiderRobot is shorter than rock
    Do in order
      spiderRobot neck move up
      spiderRobot neck move down
Else
    Do nothing
```

Translating the storyboard into program code is straightforward. First an *If* statement is created by dragging the *If/Else* tile into the editor and selecting *true* as the default condition, as was demonstrated previously in Figure 3-2-2. Then, the spiderRobot's *is shorter than* function is dragged into the editor in place of *true*, and rock is selected as the target object, as shown in Figure 3-2-4.

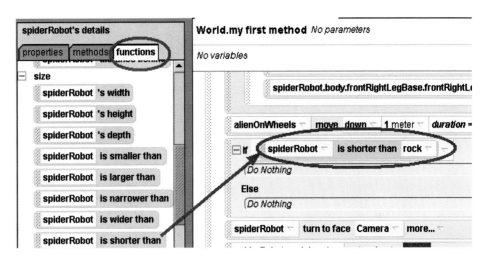

**Figure 3-2-4.** Using a function to check a condition in an *If/Else*

Finally, spiderRobot.neck *move* instructions are added in a *Do together* block for the *If* part of the *If/Else* statement. The *Else* part of the *If/Else* statement is *Do Nothing*. The resulting code is shown below.

When this code is run, a function is used to ask the question: "Is the spiderRobot shorter than the rock?" The answer is either *true* or *false* (a Boolean result). Then, a decision is made on the basis of the answer. If the answer is *true* the spiderRobot's neck moves up and down (to peek behind the rock). Otherwise, the *Else* section kicks in and nothing happens. That is, the spiderRobot's neck is not moved up and down. We could have written instructions to make the spiderRobot do something different in the *Else* part—like spin the head around—but we wanted to show that *Do Nothing* is an acceptable alternative to an action.

## Relational operators

In the example above, we used a built-in function to compare the heights of the spiderRobot and the rock. We frequently take advantage of built-in functions to check a condition in an *If* statement. Sometimes, though, we want to write our own condition using a relational operator. Alice provides six relational operators grouped together in the math category of the World's built-in functions, as shown in Figure 3-2-5. The operators work the same as they do in mathematics. We added labels to the screen capture in Figure 3-2-5 to indicate the meaning of each operator. For example, "==" means "is equal to" and "!=" means "is not equal to."

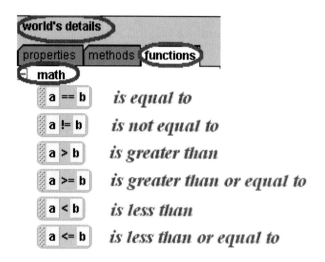

**Figure 3-2-5.** Relational operators

As an example of using a relational operator to write your own condition, let's assume that we know the rock in the First Encounter world is 2 meters tall (2 meters is about 6 feet). We could write an *If* statement that checks the spiderRobot's height against 2 meters. We want to write a statement for the following storyboard:

```
If the spiderRobot's height is less than 2 meters
    Do in order
        spiderRobot's neck move up
        spiderRobot's neck move down
```

The condition of the *If* statement is "spiderRobot-'s height is less than 2 meters." The condition must be written as a Boolean expression (is either *true* or *false*). Let's write an *If* statement for this storyboard, creating our own Boolean expression with a relational operator.

First, drag the *If* tile into the editor, as in the examples above. Then, complete the following two-step process:

1. Drag the World function "less than" tile ($a < b$) on top of the *true* tile in the *If* statement. A popup menu allows you to select values for $a$ and $b$, as shown in Figure 3-2-6.

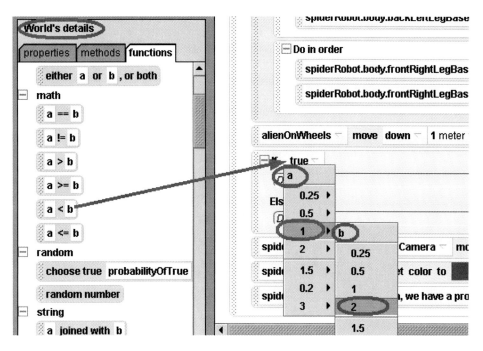

**Figure 3-2-6.**  Creating your own Boolean expression

From the popup menu, select 1 for *a* and 2 for *b*. The resulting expression looks like this:

Actually, we want to drag in the tile representing the spiderRobot's height to use as the value for *a*, but we chose 1 from the popup menu as a placeholder to complete this first step. We will fix it in the next step.

2. Now, drag in the spiderRobot's *height* function to replace the 1 (that was put there as a placeholder). Inside the *If* part, a *Do in order* block and instructions to make the spider-Robot's neck move up and down are added. The *Else* part of the statement is left as *Do nothing.* If the condition (spiderRobot's *height* < 2) is *false*, no action will be taken. The resulting code is shown below.

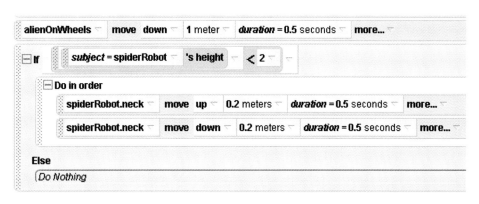

## The need for repetition

In the example world created in Chapter 3, Section 1, the spiderRobot moves forward to the rock (an expression computes the distance—several meters), and the spiderRobot's legs simulate a walking action (turning the leg joints) only once. (The code is shown in Figure 3-2-7.) When the program is run, the walking action is not realistic because the robot moves forward a relatively long distance but the legs take only one step.

**Figure 3-2-7.** The spiderRobot moves forward several meters but legs take only 1 step

It would be more realistic if the spiderRobot legs walked a step with each meter that the spiderRobot moves forward. In other words, if the spiderRobot moved forward 3 meters, then the leg walking action would occur 3 times. If the spiderRobot moved forward 4 meters, then the leg walking action would occur 4 times, and so forth.

We could revise the program code to move spiderRobot forward 1 meter and the legs would take one step. (You may recall that this is what was in the original code in Chapter 2, Section 2). Then, the code would (once again) look like the code shown in Figure 3-2-8.

**Figure 3-2-8.** The spiderRobot moves forward 1 meter and legs walk once

The problem is that the spiderRobot is now moving forward only 1 meter. We want the spiderRobot to move forward several (3 or 4) meters. It would be rather tedious to create this set of instructions 3 or 4 times. Also, think about what would happen if we wanted the robot to move forward say 20 meters!

A possible solution is to use the clipboard. The clipboard is a wonderful tool for copying a set of instructions from one place to another in the editor. (See Appendix B for instructions on how to use the clipboard.) In this situation, however, dragging the same set of instructions from the editor to the clipboard and then from the clipboard back into the editor several times is still a bit tedious.

## Repetition with a loop

What we want is a way to make our job easier by using a repetition control construct, called a *Loop* statement. A *Loop* statement, found in many programming languages, is a simple and easy way to repeat an action a counted number of times. To create a loop in a program, the *Loop* tile is dragged into the editor (drag it into the editor, before the *Do together* block), as shown in Figure 3-2-9.

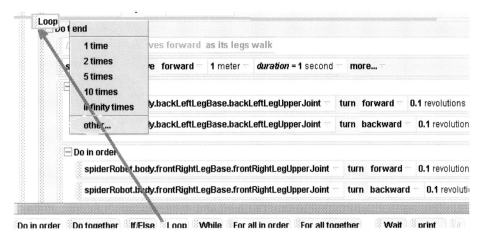

**Figure 3-2-9.**  Dragging a *Loop* statement into the editor

When the Loop tile is dragged into the editor, a popup menu offers a choice for the count (the number of times the loop will execute). Alice uses the term "end" to describe the end of the count. We selected *other* and then entered the number 3, as shown in Figure 3-2-10. Note that a loop can execute only a whole number of times. (A whole number is a number with no fractional part.)

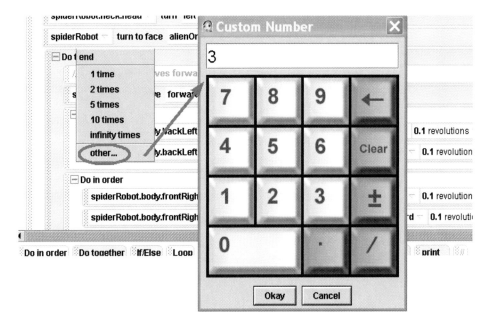

**Figure 3-2-10.**  Selecting a count for the *Loop* statement

Finally, drag the *Do together* block into the *Loop* statement, as shown in Figure 3-2-11.

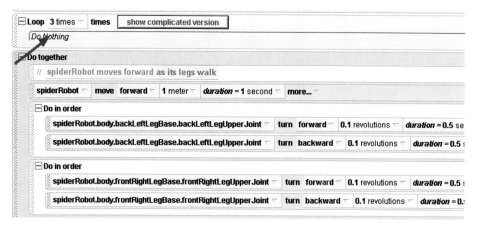

**Figure 3-2-11.** Dragging the *Do together* block of instructions into the *Loop* statement

The resulting *Loop* statement is shown in Figure 3-2-12. The blue-green block encloses all the instructions in the loop construct. The comment has been updated to show that the walking steps will be repeated 3 times.

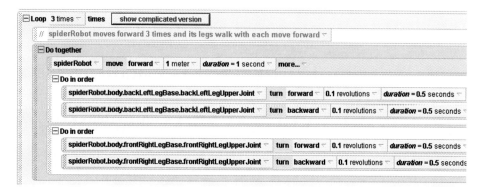

**Figure 3-2-12.** The completed *Loop* statement

# Tips & Techniques 3
## Engineering Look and Feel

 The phrase "look and feel" describes the appearance of objects. We often describe look and feel in terms of properties, such as *color* and *texture*. As an example, we might say that a sweater is "yellow and has a smooth velvety texture." The topics in this section provide information on how to modify the look and feel of a world and objects within it.

### Texture maps

Objects displayed in Alice are covered with texture maps to provide a sense of realness. For example, consider the plate (Kitchen) on a table (Furniture on CD or Web gallery) scene, shown in Figure T-3-1.

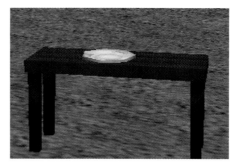

**Figure T-3-1.**  A plate on the table

A texture map named *ground.GrassTexture* covers the ground surface, and a texture map named *plate.TextureMap* covers a plate, as can be seen in Figure T-3-2.

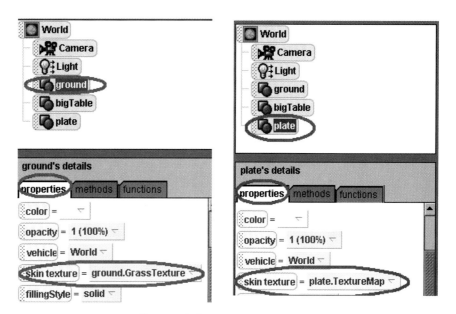

**Figure T-3-2.**  Texture maps used as skin

A graphic file (.gif, .bmp, .jpg, or .tif) can be used to give an object a different look. The Internet is a good to place to look for graphic files—just be sure the images are not copyrighted! As an example, let's change the appearance of the plate to look like a cookie instead. Two steps are required. The first step is to import a texture map that we intend to use for that object. In this example, we selected the plate object, clicked the **import texture map** button, and then selected *cookie.gif* to be used as the texture. (The *cookie.gif* file is not part of Alice. We created the graphic image using a paint program.) Figure T-3-3 illustrates the importing step. The second step is to set the skin property to use the new texture map, as in Figure T-3-4. The result is seen in Figure T-3-5.

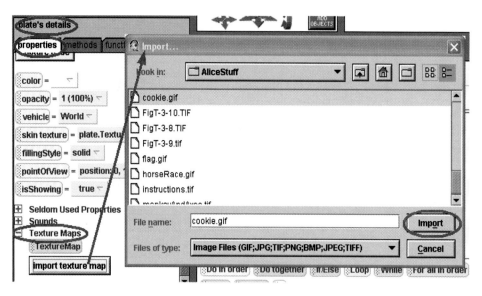

**Figure T-3-3.** Importing a texture map

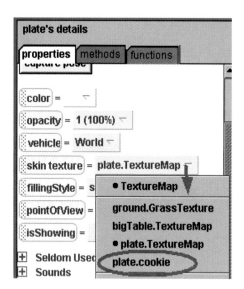

**Figure T-3-4.** Changing the texture map for the skin

**Figure T-3-5.** Cookie plate

## Special effect: fog

In some worlds you may want to create a fog-like atmosphere. Consider the scene in Figure T-3-6. A knight (Medieval) is searching for a dragon (Medieval) in a forest (trees in Nature folder). We would like to give the impression that the dragon is hiding from the knight. In most stories involving dragons, the weather is dreary and grey. Some sort of fog would make the knight's job (of finding the dragon) much more challenging.

**Figure T-3-6.** No fog

To add fog, click on *World* in the object-tree and select properties, as shown in Figure T-3-7. Then, click on the image to the right of *fogStyle* and select *density*. Density refers to the thickness of the fog. To adjust the fog density, click the *fogDensity* tile and adjust the density value to achieve the desired effect. A larger density value produces a thicker fog.

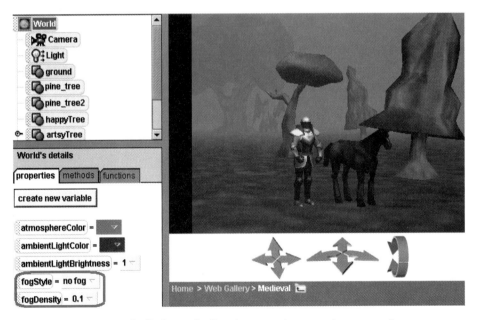

**Figure T-3-7.** The *fogStyle* and *fogDensity* properties are used to create a foggy scene

## Exercises

### 3-1 Exercises

1. *Robot to Lunar Lander*

   Use the First Encounter world to recreate the program code as described in Chapter 3, Section 1. After the spiderRobot moves to the rock, have the spiderRobot turn to face the lunarLander and then move forward half the distance between the spiderRobot and the lunarLander.

2. *Dog to Fire Hydrant*

   Create a world with a dog (wolf from Animals) and a fire hydrant (City), as shown in the scene below. (We used a wolf as a dog.) Write an instruction that puts together a *distance to* function and a math expression to move the dog to the fire hydrant. The dog should stop short of colliding with the hydrant.

3. *Hop*

   Create a world with a crate (Objects) and a kangaroo (Animals). Write a program to make the kangaroo hop to the top of the box, turning the kangaroo's legs backward and forward to make it look like a hop. Use the *height* function to guide the forward and upward movements.

4. *Volleyball Jump*

   Create a new world with a volleyball net, a volleyball (Sports), and the skater girl and girl (People), as shown below. Each person in the world is likely to have a different height and athletic ability. Let's assume each person can jump up 1/4 of his or her height to hit the volleyball. Write instructions to make each person jump up this distance and then move back down the same distance. Call the built-in *height* function and use an expression to compute the distance the person should move up and down.

## 3-2 Exercises

5. *SpiderRobot's Walk*

In Section 3-2, program code was presented to make the spiderRobot walk forward 3 times in a loop. Recreate the program code and test the *Loop* statement with a count of 2, 4, and then 5. Which count works best? Why?

6. *Blimp and Dragon*

Create a scene as shown below with a blimp (Vehicle) and a dragon (Medieval). In this fantasy scene, the dragon has found a blimp and is curious. The dragon flies around the blimp to check it out. Write a program to have the dragon move to the blimp and then fly around it (lengthwise) three times.

7. *Snowman to Stool*

This exercise uses a number function as the count for a *Loop*. Create a world with a snowman and a stool, as seen below. Use a *Loop* to make the snowman (People) move to the stool (Kitchen), one meter at a time. Use a *distance to* function to determine the number of times the loop repeats. (The *distance to* function might return a fractional distance such as 3.75 meters. The *Loop* statement truncates the fractional number to the integer 3 and will repeat 3 times.) We recommend that you test your solution by moving the snowman and the stool to different locations on the screen and running the program with each change, so you can whether it works no matter where the snowman and the stool are located.

## Summary

In this chapter, we looked at how to put together the "pieces" of program code. The "pieces" that we use to create our programs include the following:

> **instruction**—a statement that executes to make objects perform a certain action
> **control structure**—a statement that controls the execution of instructions
> **function**—asks a question about a condition or computes a value
> **expression**—a math operation on numbers or other kinds of values

Alice provides built-in functions for the World and for objects within it. Functions can have different types of values (for example, number, Boolean, or object). Expressions allow you to compute a value or perform a comparison of some property of two objects. One use of functions and expressions in an animation program is to help avoid collisions (when an object moves into the same position as another object).

We can use the built-in functions and Boolean expressions (expressions that have a *true* or *false* value) to check the current condition in the world and make decisions about whether (or not) a section of the program will be executed. In Alice, the conditional execution control structure is the *If/Else* statement. An *If* statement has two parts: the *If* part and the *Else* part. In the *If* part, a condition is checked and a decision is made depending on the condition. If the condition is *true*, the *If* part of the *If/Else* statement is executed. Otherwise, the *Else* part of the statement is executed. It is possible that the *Else* part of the statement may be *Do nothing*, in which case no action is taken. (It is also possible for the *If* part of the statement to be *Do nothing*—but this is an awkward way of thinking about a condition.)

A simple repetition control structure is the *Loop*. A *Loop* statement allows you to repeat a section of program code a counted number of times.

### Important concepts in this chapter

- Functions can be used in Alice to ask questions about properties of the World or properties of an object within it. Functions can also be used to compute a value.
- When a function is called, it returns a particular type of value.
- A Boolean function returns either *true* or *false*.
- An expression may use an arithmetic operation (addition, subtraction, multiplication, division) to compute a numeric value.
- Another kind of expression compares one object to another, using relational operators $(==, !=, >, >=, <, <=)$. The result is *true* or *false*.
- A conditional execution control structure (in Alice, an *If/Else* statement) is used to make a decision about whether a particular section of the program will be executed.
- A repetition control structure is used to repeat a section of program code again and again. A simple repetition control in Alice is the *Loop* statement.

# Part II
# Object-Oriented and Event-Driven Programming Concepts

# Chapter 4

# Classes, Objects, Methods, and Parameters

*"The Queen of Hearts, she made some tarts,*
*All on a summer day:*
*The Knave of Hearts, he stole those tarts,*
*And took them quite away!"*

---

*Instructions for Making a Strawberry Tart*
1 crust, baked
3 cups strawberries, hulled
1 pkg. strawberry gelatin
$1\frac{1}{2}$ cups of water
2 Tbs. corn starch
Place strawberries in the crust.
Mix gelatin, water, and corn starch in a small pan.
Stir, while heating to a boil.
Let cool and then pour over strawberries.
Chill.

---

When you created your own animations in earlier chapters, you may have started to think about more complicated scenarios with more twists and turns in the storyline, perhaps games or simulations. Naturally, as the storyline becomes more intricate, so does the program code for creating the animation. The program code can quickly increase to many, many lines—sort of an "explosion" in program size and complexity. Animation programs are not alone in this complexity. Real-world software applications can have thousands, even millions, of lines of code. How does a programmer deal with huge amounts of program code? One technique is to divide a very large program into manageable "pieces," making it easier to design and think about. Smaller pieces are also easier to read and debug. Object-oriented programming uses classes, objects, and methods as basic program components, which will help you organize large programs into small manageable pieces. In this chapter and the next, you will learn how to write more intricate and impressive programs by using objects (instances of classes) and writing your own methods.

## Classes

A class defines a particular kind of object. In Alice, classes are predefined as 3D models provided in the gallery, categorized into groups such as Animals, People, Buildings, Sets and Scenes, Space, and so on. Figure 4-0-1 shows some of the classes in the Animals folder. Notice that the name of a class begins with a capital letter.

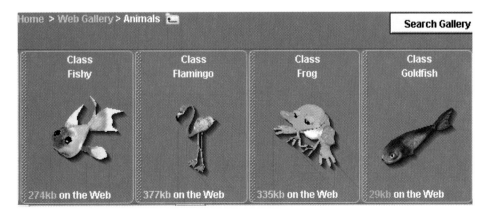

**Figure 4-0-1.** Classes of 3D Models in the Animals folder

71

Each class is a blueprint that tells Alice exactly how to create and display an object from that class. When an object is created and displayed, we call this instantiating the class because an object is an instance of that class.

## Objects

In Figure 4-0-2, Person and Dog are classes. Joe, stan, and cindy are instances of the Person class while spike, scamp, and fido are instances of the Dog class. Notice that the name of an object begins with a lowercase letter. This naming style helps us to easily distinguish the name of a class from the name of an object. All objects of the same class share some commonality. All Person objects have properties such as two legs, two arms, height, and eye color. Person objects can perform walking and speaking actions. All Dog objects have properties including four legs, height, and fur-color, and have the ability to run and bark. Although each object belongs to a class, it is still unique in its own way. Joe is tall and has green eyes. Cindy is short and has blue eyes. Spike has brown fur and his bark is a low growl, and scamp has golden-color fur and his bark is a high-pitched yip.

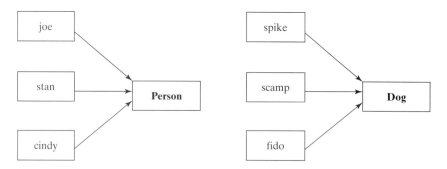

**Figure 4-0-2.** Organizing objects into classes

In Figure 4-0-3, larry, lila, and louis are all instances of the Lemur class (Animals) in Alice. We named the lemurs in this world, made them different heights, and changed the color of lila. Larry, lila and louis are all objects of the same Lemur character class and have many common characteristics. They also differ in that larry is the tallest, lila has rich, dark fur, and louis is the shortest.

**Figure 4-0-3.** Objects of the Lemur class in Alice

## Methods

A method is a coordinated sequence of instructions that will be carried out when requested. You have already used methods in your animations. Every object in an Alice world has a repertoire of instructions it knows how to do—*move, turn, turn to face*, etc. These instructions are actually primitive methods, built-in to the Alice software. The primitive methods can be organized into a method of your own—to carry out a small piece of the overall program. Each method performs its own job, but all the methods in a program work together to create the overall animation.

As your animation programs grow larger, it will become increasingly important to use many, many methods as a way of organizing the program. Methods divide a program into small manageable pieces that work together to create a meaningful whole. Just as paragraphs, sections, and chapters make a book easier to read, methods make a program easier to read. Methods also provide a number of advantages. For example, once a method is written it allows us to think about an overall task instead of all the small actions that were needed to complete the task. This is called abstraction.

Some methods need to be sent certain pieces of information to carry out an action. For example a *move* method needs a *direction* (*forward, backward, left, right, up,* or *down*) and a *distance* (in meters). A parameter acts like a basket to receive information that we send to a method. In a way, you can think of a method as somewhat like a recipe—a set of instructions that describe how to perform some action. (As an example, see the recipe at the beginning of this chapter for making a strawberry tart.) Parameters hold onto the specific items of information. In a recipe, a parameter could specify the amount of water. In a method, a parameter could specify the distance a spaceship is to move.

In Alice, you can define methods for an object acting alone or for two or more objects interacting with one another. This is similar to the way a director works with the cast of actors in a play. The director gives instructions sometimes to a single cast member and at other times to several cast members to coordinate their actions. Methods that specifically reference more than one object are world-level methods. Methods that define behaviors for a single object may be considered class-level methods.

Section 4-1 presents an introduction to class-level methods. An advantage of class-level methods is that once new methods are defined, we can create a new class with all the new methods (and also the old methods) as available actions. This is a form of inheritance—the new class inherits methods from the old class.

## 4-1 Class-level methods and inheritance

The galleries of 3D models in Alice give us a choice of diverse and well-designed classes of objects for populating and creating a scenic backdrop in a virtual world. When you add an instance of a 3D model to an Alice world, it already "knows" how to perform a set of methods—*move, turn, roll,* and *resize* (to name a few). The 3D model class already defines these methods. After writing several programs, it is natural to think about extending the actions an object "knows" how to perform.

In this section, you will learn how to write new methods that define new actions to be carried out by an object acting alone (rather than several objects acting together). We call these class-level methods. Class-level methods are rather special, because we can save an object along with its newly defined method(s) as a new kind of object. In Alice, the new kind of object is saved as a new 3D class model. Later instances of the new class still know how to perform all the actions defined in the original class but will also be able to perform all the actions in the newly defined methods. We say that the new class inherits all the properties and methods of the original class.

### Example

Consider the iceSkater shown in the winter scene of Figure 4-1-1. (The IceSkater class is from the People collection, and the Lake class is from the Environments collection in the gallery.)

**Figure 4-1-1.** The iceSkater

We want the skater to perform typical figure-skating actions. She is dressed in a skating costume and is wearing ice skates, but this does not mean she knows how to skate. However, all Alice objects "know" how to perform simple methods such as *move, turn*, and *roll*. We can use a combination of these simple methods to "teach" the ice skater how to perform a more complex action. We begin with a method to make the skater perform a skating motion.

## A Class-Level Method

Skating movements are complex actions that require several motion instructions involving various parts of the body. (Professional animators at Disney and Pixar may spend many, many hours observing the movement of various parts of the human body so as to create realistic animations.) To skate, a skater slides forward on the left leg and then slides forward on the right leg. Of course, the entire skater body is moving forward as the legs perform the sliding movements. The steps in a skating action are put together as a sequence of motions in a storyboard, as shown next.

```
skate

Do together
Move skater forward 2 meters
    Do in order
        slide on left leg
        slide on right leg
```

Notice that the storyboard breaks down the skating action into two pieces—slide on the left leg and slide on the right leg. The sliding motions can each be broken down into simpler methods. Breaking a complex action down into simpler actions is called refinement. Here we are using a design technique known as stepwise refinement. We first describe general actions, and then break each action down into smaller and smaller steps (successively refined) until the whole task is defined in simple actions. Each piece contributes a small part to the overall animation; the pieces together accomplish the entire task.

The following diagram illustrates the refinement of the *slideLeft* and *slideRight* actions. The actions needed to slide on the left leg are to lift the right leg and turn the upper body slightly forward. Then, lower the right leg and turn the upper body backward (to an upright position). Similar actions are carried out to slide on the right leg.

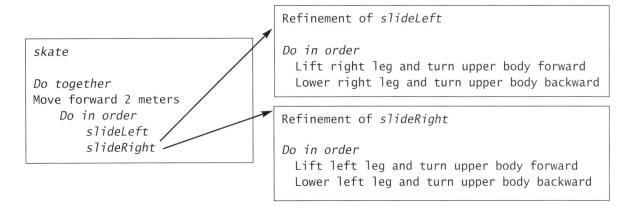

```
skate

Do together
Move forward 2 meters
    Do in order
        slideLeft
        slideRight
```

```
Refinement of slideLeft

Do in order
  Lift right leg and turn upper body forward
  Lower right leg and turn upper body backward
```

```
Refinement of slideRight

Do in order
  Lift left leg and turn upper body forward
  Lower left leg and turn upper body backward
```

Nothing else needs to be refined. We are now ready to translate the design into program code. We could translate this design to instructions in just the one method, but it would be lengthy. Furthermore, you can quickly see that we have used stepwise refinement to break the skate task down into distinct pieces. So, we will demonstrate how to write several small methods and make them work together to accomplish a larger task.

Skate is a complex action that is designed specifically for the iceSkater and involves no other objects. Likewise, the *slideLeft* and *slideRight* actions are designed specifically for the iceSkater. The methods should be written as class-level methods because they involve only the ice skater. We begin with the *slideLeft* method. The iceSkater is selected in the Object tree and the **create new method** button is clicked in the details panel. In the New Method popup window, enter *slideLeft* as the name of the new method. The left side of Figure 4-1-2 illustrates this first step. Click on the OK button. The code editor opens a new panel where the program code can be created. The right side of Figure 4-1-2 shows the method name and the new panel in the code editor.

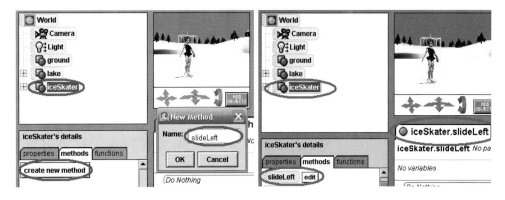

**Figure 4-1-2.** A *slideLeft* class-level method

To implement the *slideLeft* method, we enter instructions in the editor. The idea is to translate the design into actual program instructions. For example, to translate the design steps for sliding on the left leg, we use the following:

| Design step | Instruction |
|---|---|
| Lift the right leg | *turn* the rightLeg forward |
| Turn upper body forward | *turn* the upperBody forward |
| (We inserted a short *wait* to allow time for forward movement.) | |
| Lower the right leg | *turn* the rightLeg backward |
| Turn the upper body backward | *turn* the upperBody backward |

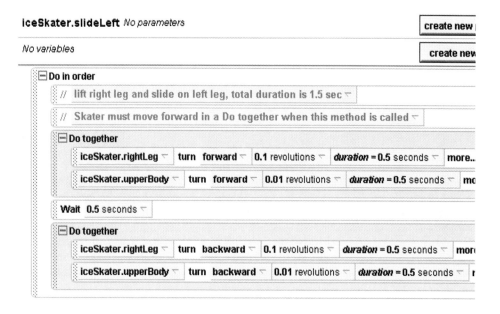

**Figure 4-1-3.** The *slideLeft* method

Figure 4-1-3 illustrates translating the textual storyboard into instructions for sliding on the left leg. The instructions for sliding forward on the right leg are similar. So, writing the *slideRight* method is rather easy. Figure 4-1-4 illustrates translating the textual storyboard into instructions to slide forward on the right leg.

With the *slideLeft* and *slideRight* methods written, we are now ready to write the *skate* method. The *skate* method is really quite simple: *slideLeft* and then *slideRight* at the same time as the entire skater is moving forward. To create the *skate* method, the *slideLeft* and *slideRight*

**Figure 4-1-4.** The *slideRight* method

methods are dragged into the editor (using the same drag-and-drop technique as previously used to create instructions for built-in methods such as *move*, *turn*, and *roll*. Figure 4-1-5 illustrates dragging the *slideLeft* and *slideRight* method tiles into the editor for the *skate* method. The skate method moves the skater forward and calls the *slideLeft* method and then calls the *slideRight* method. Note that the calls to the *slideLeft* and *slideRight* methods are enclosed in a *Do in order* block, nested within a *Do together*. The *Do together* block is needed to ensure that the instruction that moves the skater forward is performed simultaneously with the left and right sliding motions. The duration of the forward movement of the skater is the sum of the durations of the left and right slides. Paying attention to the durations of the instructions in a *Do together* block will help coordinate the motions to begin and end at the same time. Figure 4-1-5 illustrates the completed *skate m*ethod.

If the **Play** button is clicked at this time, the animation will NOT run. Althugh the *skate* method has been defined, Alice has not been told to execute it. That is, the method has not been called into action. To call the *skate* method into action, it is necessary to drag the *skate* method tile into *world.my first* **method**. When the *skate* method is called, the skater glides forward in a realistic motion.

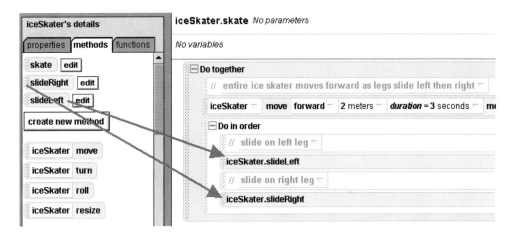

**Figure 4-1-5.** The *skate* method

## A second example—using a parameter

The forward skate motion is truly impressive! Building on this success, let's write a second method to make the ice skater perform a spin. Once again, we will need to write several methods that work together to complete a complex action. In a spin, the ice skater should spin (turn around) several times.

A spin maneuver generally has three parts, the preparation for the spin, the spin itself, and the end of the spin (to finish the spin). In preparation for the spin, the skater's arms and legs change position to provide the strength needed to propel her body around. Then the skater spins around. After the spin, the arms and legs should be repositioned to where they were before the spin. A *spin* method is likely to have the skater turn several revolutions. We don't know exactly how many times the skater might turn. This is an example of a method where a parameter can be helpful. A parameter allows you to send information to a method when the method is called. You have been using parameters all along. Most built-in methods have parameters that allow you to send information to the method. For example, a *move* instruction has parameters that allow you to send in the direction, distance, and duration. We say that the values are sent in as arguments to the parameters. A parameter, *howManyTimes,* is needed to specify the number of times the ice skater will spin around. The storyboard is shown next.

```
spin

Parameter: howManyTimes
Do in order
    prepare to spin
    spin the skater around howManyTimes
    finish the spin
```

We can use stepwise refinement to design the simple steps for each part of the spin. The "prepare to spin" step can be written as a method (*prepareToSpin*) where the skater's arms move up and one leg turns. The "finish spin" step can also be written as a method (*finishSpin*) to move the arms and legs back to their original positions, prior to the spin. The following diagram illustrates a refinement of the *spin* method.

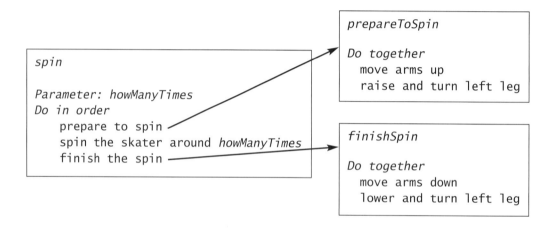

Nothing else needs to be refined. We are now ready to translate the design into program code. Once again, class-level methods should be used, because we are defining a complex motion specifically for the ice skater.

Figure 4-1-6 illustrates the *prepareToSpin* method, where the ice skater raises her left leg as she lifts her arms.

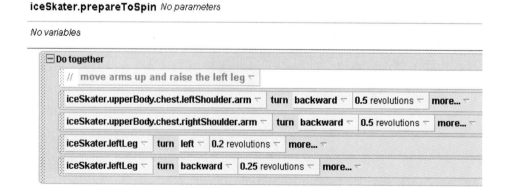

**Figure 4-1-6.** The *prepareToSpin* method to raise arms and one leg

Figure 4-1-7 presents the *finishSpin* method to reposition the skater's arms and leg to their original positions at the end of her spin.

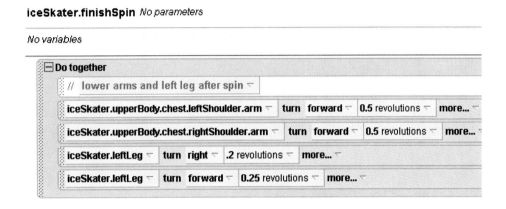

**Figure 4-1-7.** The *finishSpin* method to lower arms and leg

Now that *prepareToSpin* and *finishSpin* have been written, the *spin* method can be created. A **create new parameter** button automatically appears in the upper right hand corner of the editor. When the **create new parameter** button is clicked, a dialog box pops up, as illustrated in Figure 4-1-8. The name of a parameter is entered and its *type* is selected. The *type* of a parameter can be a *Number*, *Boolean* ("true" or "false"), *Object*, or *Other* (for example, a color or sound). The *howManySpins* parameter is a number that specifies how many times the skater is to turn around (1 revolution is 1 complete spin around). The order in which the methods are called is important so as to adjust the skater's arms and legs in preparation for the spin and after the spin. The completed *spin* method is illustrated in Figure 4-1-9.

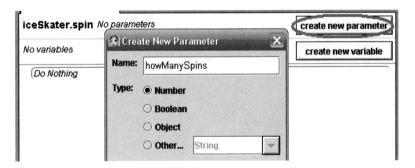

**Figure 4-1-8.** Creating a new parameter in the *spin* method

The code for the two examples above (the *skate* and *spin* methods) is a bit longer than we have written in previous chapters. It is important that the code is easy to understand, because we have carefully broken down the overall task into smaller methods. The small methods all work together to complete the overall action. Also, the methods have been well documented, with comments that tell us what the method accomplishes. Good design and comments make our code easier to understand as well as easier to write and debug.

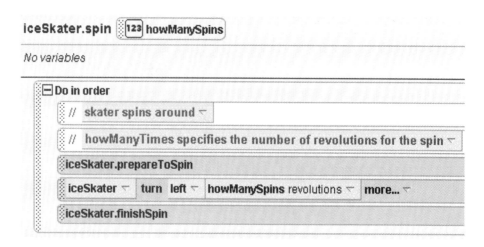

**Figure 4-1-9.** The *spin* method

### Creating a new class

The iceSkater now has two class-level methods, *skate* and *spin*. (She also has several smaller class-level methods that implement small pieces of the *skate* and *spin* methods.) Writing and testing the methods took some time and effort to achieve. It would be a shame to put all this work into one world and not be able to use it again in another animation program we might create later. We would like to save the iceSkater and her newly defined methods so we can use them in another world (we won't need to write these methods again for another animation program). To do this, the *iceSkater* must be saved out as a new 3D model (class).

Saving the iceSkater (with her newly defined methods) as a new class is a two-step process. The first step is to rename the iceSkater. This is an IMPORTANT STEP! We want Alice to save this new class with a different 3D filename than the original IceSkater class. To rename an object, right-click on the name of the object in the Object tree, select *rename* from the popup menu, and enter the new name in the box. In this example, we right-clicked on iceSkater in the Object tree and changed the name to cleverSkater, as shown in Figure 4-1-10.

The second step is to save out as a new class: right click on cleverSkater in the Object tree and this time select *save object*. In the Save Object popup box, navigate to the folder/directory where you wish to save the new class, as in Figure 4-1-11, and then click the Save button.

**Figure 4-1-10.** Renaming iceSkater as cleverSkater

The class is automatically named with the new name, beginning with a capital letter and a file-name extension .a2c, which stands for "Alice version 2.0 Class" (just as the .a2w extension in a world filename stands for "Alice version 2.0 World").

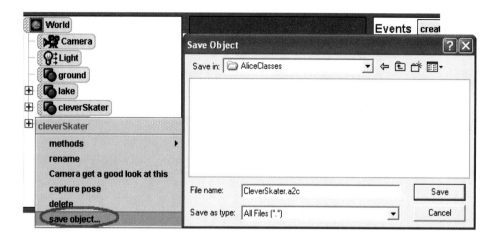

**Figure 4-1-11.**  Save Object dialog box

Once a new class has been created, it can be used in a new world by selecting **Import** from the **File** menu, as illustrated in Figure 4-1-12. When an instance of the CleverSkater class is added to a world, she will be just like an instance of the IceSkater class, except that a cleverSkater object knows how to *skate* and *spin* in addition to all of the methods an iceSkater object can perform.

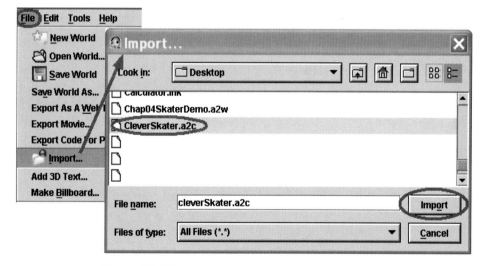

**Figure 4-1-12.**  Importing a new object from a saved-out class

## Inheritance—benefits

Creating a new class based on a previously defined class is called inheritance. Inheritance in most object-oriented languages is more complicated than in Alice. The basic idea is the same—adding functionality by defining new methods for a new kind of inherited class. Inheritance is considered one of the strengths of object-oriented programming because it allows you to write code once and reuse it in other programs.

Another benefit of creating new classes is the ability to share code with others in team projects. For example, if you are working on an Alice project as a team, each person can write class-level methods for an object in the world. Then, each team member can save out the new class. Objects of the new classes are added to a single team-constructed world for a shared project. This is a benefit we cannot overemphasize. In the "real world," computer professionals generally work on team projects. Cooperatively developed software is often the way professional animation teams at animation studios work.

## Guidelines for Writing Class-Level Methods

Class-level methods are a powerful feature of Alice. Of course, with power there is also some danger. To avoid potential misuse of class-level methods, we offer some guidelines.

1. Do create many different class-level methods. They are extremely useful and helpful. Some classes in Alice already have a few class-level methods defined. For example, the Lion class has methods *startStance, walkForward, completeWalk, roar,* and *charge.* Figure 4-1-13 shows a thumbnail image for the Lion class (from the Web gallery), including its class-level methods and sounds.

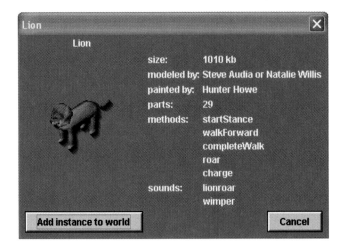

**Figure 4-1-13.** Class-level methods and sounds for the Lion class

2. Play a sound in a class-level method **ONLY IF** the sound has been imported for the object (instead of the world). If the sound has been imported for the object and the object is saved out as a new class, the sound is saved out with the object. Then the sound can be played anywhere in any world where an object of this class is added. On the other hand, if the sound is imported for the world, the sound is not saved out with the object and you cannot depend on the sound being available in other worlds.

3. Do not use instructions for other objects from within a class-level method. Class-level methods are clearly defined for a specific class. We expect to save out the object as a new class and reuse it in a later world. We cannot depend on other objects being present in other programs in other worlds. For example, a penguin (Animals) is added to the winter scene, as in Figure 4-1-14. We write a class-level method named *skateAround,* where the penguin object is

**Figure 4-1-14.** The skater will skate around the penguin

specifically named in two of the instructions (circled in Figure 4-1-15). If the cleverSkater with the *skateAround* method is saved out as a new class and then a cleverSkater object is added to a later world where no penguin exists, Alice will open an Error dialog box to tell you about a missing object. The error would be that the cleverSkater cannot skate around a penguin that does not exist in the world!

**Note:** Possible exceptions to guideline #4 are the world and camera objects, which are always present.

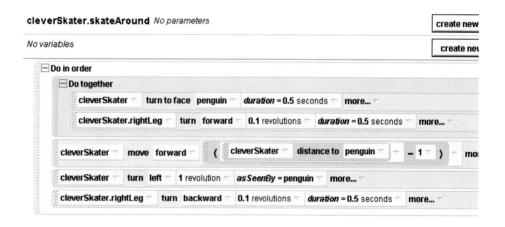

**Figure 4-1-15.** Bad example: instructions specifying another object in a class-level method

## A class-level method with an object parameter

What if you would like to write a class-level method where another object is involved? The solution is to use an object parameter in the class-level method. Let's use the same example as above, where we want a cleverSkater to skate around another object. The *skateAround* method can be modified to use a parameter, arbitrarily named *whichObject*, as shown in Figure 4-1-16. The *whichObject* parameter is only a placeholder, not an actual object, so we do not have to worry about a particular object (like the penguin) having to be in another world. Alice will not allow the *skateAround* method to be called without passing in an object to the *whichObject* parameter. So, we can be sure that some sort of object will be there to skate around.

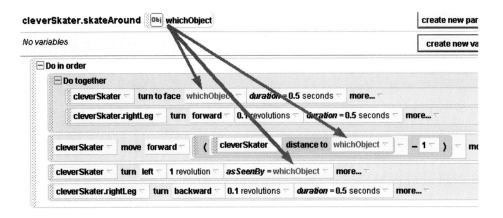

**Figure 4-1-16.** Using an object parameter in a class-level method

## Testing

Once you have created and saved out a new class, it should be tested in a new world. The initial scene was shown in Figure 4-1-17. A sample test program is presented in Figure 4-1-17. In this test, we have called the *skate, spin,* and *skateAround* methods to test each method.

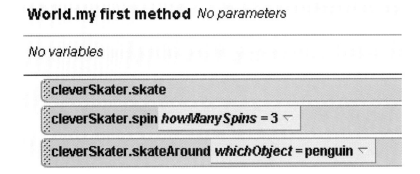

**Figure 4-1-17.** A sample program

## Tips & Techniques 4
### Visible and Invisible Objects

 Properties of objects are sometimes used in games and simulations to achieve a special effect, such as making an object visible or invisible. In this section we look at techniques and examples of changing the visibility of objects.

### The opacity property

The following example changes the opacity of a fish in an ocean world. (Opacity is how opaque something is: how hard it is to see through.) Figure T-4-1 shows an aquatic scene. This world is easily created by adding an oceanFloor (Ocean) and a lilfish (Ocean). (Optional items— seaweed and fireCoral were added from the OceanFloor folder in the CD or Web gallery.)

The lilfish is swimming out to lunch, and her favorite seafood is seaweed. Instructions to point lilfish at the seaweed and then swim toward it are shown in Figure T-4-2. The *wiggletail* instruction is a method, shown in Figure T-4-2(b), that makes the fish wiggle its tail in a left-right motion.

As the fish moves toward the seaweed, she will also move away from the camera. So she should fade, because water blurs our vision of distant objects. We can make lilfish become

**Figure T-4-1.** An ocean floor scene with lilfish

**Figure T-4-2(a).** Code to make lilfish swim toward the seaweed

**Figure T-4-2(b).** The *wiggletail* method

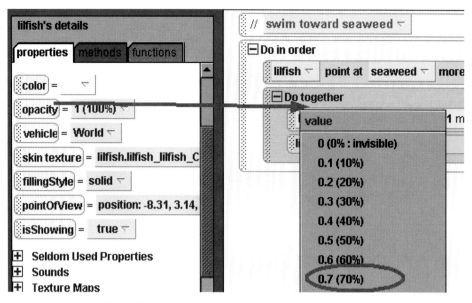

**Figure T-4-3.**  Dragging the *opacity* tile into code editor

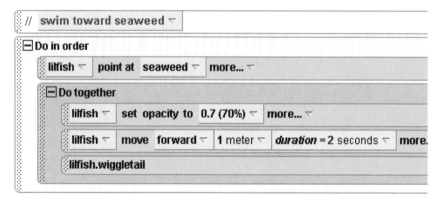

**Figure T-4-4.**  Code now includes a *set opacity* instruction

less visible by changing the opacity property. As opacity is decreased, an object becomes less distinct (more difficult to see). To write an instruction to change the opacity, click on the lilfish's properties tab and drag the *opacity* tile into the editor. From the popup menu, select the *opacity* percentage, as shown in Figure T-4-3.

The resulting code is in Figure T-4-4.

When the world is run, lilfish will become less visible, as shown in Figure T-4-5. At 0% opacity, an object will totally disappear. This does not mean that the object has been deleted; it is still part of the world but is not visible on the screen.

## The isShowing property

Each object has a property called *isShowing*. At the time an object is first added to a world, the object is made visible in the scene and *isShowing* is set to *true*. Changing the value of this property is especially useful in game like programs where you want to signal the end of a game. Figure T-4-6 illustrates the *isShowing* property as *true* for "You won!" Setting *isShowing* to *false* makes the "You won!" text invisible, as shown in Figure T-4-7. (For this world, we used the bottleThrow object from the Amusement Park folder in the CD or Web gallery.)

**Figure T-4-5.** The lilfish becomes more difficult to see as *opacity* is decreased

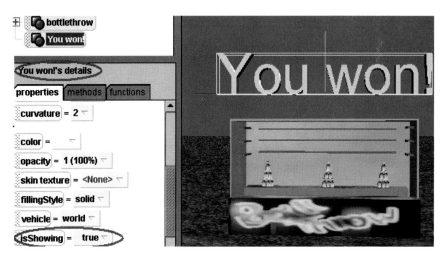

**Figure T-4-6.** The *isShowing* property is *true* and "You won!" is visible

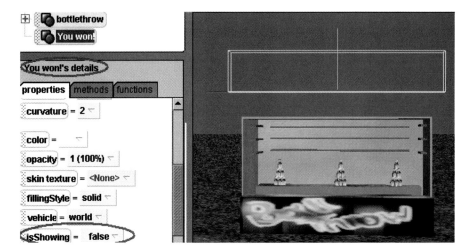

**Figure T-4-7.** The *isShowing* property is *false* and "You won!" is not visible

When its *isShowing* property is set to *false*, the object is not removed from the world; it is simply not displayed on the screen. The object can be made to "reappear" by setting its *isShowing* property back to *true*.

In this example, we want the text to appear when the player wins the game. To create an instruction that sets the *isShowing* property to *true*, drag the *isShowing* property tile into the world and select *true* from the popup menu. The result is shown in Figure T-4-8.

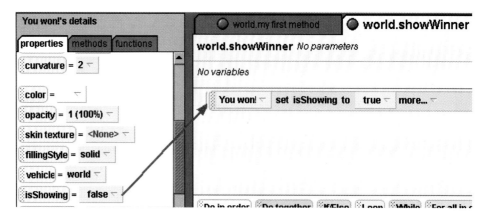

**Figure T-4-8.** An instruction to set *isShowing* to *true* at runtime

### Relationship of *isShowing* and *opacity* properties

The *isShowing* and *opacity* properties track different (though related) states of an object. The *isShowing* property is strictly *true* or *false*—like a light switch that can be either on or off. *Opacity* is a sliding scale—like a dimmer switch that can adjust the brightness of a light. Though it is true that when *opacity* is 0%, the object is invisible, nonetheless when you make an object have an *opacity* of 0%, Alice does not automatically make *isShowing false*. Likewise, when you make *isShowing false*, Alice does not automatically make *opacity* 0%.

A good piece of advice is: "Be consistent." If you are using *isShowing* in your program to set the visibility, then do not use *opacity* to check whether the object is visible. Likewise, if you are using *opacity* to set the visibility, do not use *isShowing* to check whether the object is visible.

## Exercises

### 4-1 Exercises

1. *Enhanced cleverSkater*
   Create an even better cleverSkater than the one presented in Section 4-1. In addition to the *skateForward*, *spin*, and *skateAround* methods, create *skateBackward* and *jump* class-level methods. In *skateBackward*, the skater should perform similar actions to those in the *skateForward* method, but slide backward instead of forward. In a *jump* method, the skater should move forward, lift one leg, then move upward (in the air) and back down to land gracefully on the ice and lower her leg back to its starting position. Save out your enhanced skater as EnhancedCleverSkater.
   Test your newly defined class by starting a new world with a frozen lake. Add an enhancedCleverSkater to the world. Also, add a penguin and a duck.

   (a) Call each of the methods you have written.
   (b) Then call the *skateAround* method—to make the skater skate around the penguin and then the duck. (This will require two calls to the *skateAround* method.)

2. *Lock Combination*

   Create a world with a comboLock (Objects folder). Create four class-level methods—*leftOne, rightOne, leftRevolution,* and *rightRevolution*— that turn the dial 1 number left, 1 number right, 1 revolution left, and 1 revolution right, respectively. Then, create a class-level method named *open* that opens and another named *close* that closes the lock.

   **Hints:** One position on the dial is actually 1/40 of a revolution. Use the *endGently* style to make the motion more realistic.) Rename comboLock as TurningComboLock and save it as a new class.

3. *Funky Chicken Dance*

   Starting with a basic chicken, create a class-level method *walk* that will have the chicken perform a realistic stepping motion consisting of a left step followed by a right step. Create a second method to make the chicken perform a *funkyChicken* dance, where the chicken walks and twists its body in all different directions! Save the chicken as a new class named CoolChicken. Create a new world and add a coolChicken to the world. In *my first method*, call the *walk* and *funkyChicken* methods. Play a sound file or use a *say* instruction to accompany the funky chicken dance animation.

4. *Ninja Practice*

   Create a world with an evilNinja (People) and write class methods for traditional Ninja moves. For example, you can write *rightJab* and *leftJab* (where the Ninja jabs his hand upward with the appropriate hand), *kickLeft* and *kickRight* (where he kicks with the appropriate leg), and *leftSpin* and *rightSpin* (where he does a spin in the appropriate direction). Each method must contain more than one instruction. For example, in the *kickLeft* method, the left lower leg should turn and the foot twist at the same time as the entire leg kicks out to the left. Save the Ninja as a new class named TrainedNinja. Start a new world and add two trainedNinja objects. Create an animation where the two trainedNinja objects practice their moves, facing one another.

## Summary

In this chapter we looked at how to write our own methods and how to use parameters to send information to a method when it is called. An advantage of using methods is that the programmer can think about a collection of instructions as all one action—abstraction. Also, methods make it easier to debug our code.

Parameters are used to communicate values from one method to another. In a method, a parameter acts as a placeholder for a value of a particular type. The values sent in to a method are known as arguments. When an argument is sent in to a method, the parameter represents that argument in the instructions in the method. Examples presented in this chapter included object, sound, string, and number parameters. Parameters allow you to write one method but use it several times with different objects, sounds, numbers, and other types of values.

In a way, class-level methods can be thought of as extending an object's behavior. Once new class-level methods are defined, a new class can be saved out. The new class has a different name and has all the new methods (and also the old methods) as available actions. It inherits the properties and actions of the original class but defines more things than the original class. A major benefit is that you can use objects of the new class over and over again in new worlds. This allows you to take advantage of the methods you have written without having to write them again.

Stepwise refinement is a design technique where a complex task is broken down into small pieces and then each piece is broken down further—until the entire task is completely defined by simple actions. The simple actions all work together to carry out the complex task.

### Important concepts in this chapter

- To run (or execute) a method, the method must be called.
- Parameters are used for communication with a method.
- In a call to a method, a value sent in to a method parameter is an argument.
- A parameter must be declared to represent a value of a particular type. Types of values for parameters include object, Boolean ("true" or "false"), number, sound, color, string, and others.
- A new class can be created by defining class-level methods and then saving out the class with a new name.
- Inheritance is an object-oriented concept where a new class is defined based on an existing class.
- Class-level methods can be written that accept object parameters. This allows you to write a class-level method and pass in another object. Then, the object performing the class-level method can interact with the parameterized object.

Chapter **5**

# Interaction: Events and Event Handling

*Alice laughed, "There's no use trying," she said, "one can't believe impossible things." "I daresay you haven't had much practice," said the Queen. "When I was your age, I always did it for half-an-hour a day. Why, sometimes I've believed as many as six impossible things before breakfast."*

The real world around us is interactive. A conversation, as between Alice and the Queen above, is a "give and take" form of interaction. As we interact with objects in our world, we often give directions to them. For example, we change the channel on a television set by sending a signal from a remote control. We press a button on a game controller to make a character in a video game jump out of the way of danger.

We have concentrated on writing programs that were not interactive—we watched the objects perform actions in a movie-style animation. It's time we looked at how to create interactive programs in Alice—where the objects in the scenes respond to mouse clicks and key presses. In this chapter we will see how programs can be made interactive.

Much of computer programming (and the movie-style animations seen earlier) is computer-centric. That is, the computer program basically runs as the programmer has intended it. The programmer sets the order of actions and controls the program flow. However, many computer programs today are user-centric. In other words, it is the computer user (rather than the programmer) who determines the order of actions. The user clicks the mouse or presses a key on the keyboard to send a signal to Alice about what to do next. The mouse click or key press is an event. An event is something that happens. In response to an event, an action (or a sequence of many actions) is carried out. We say the event triggers a response.

Section 5-1 focuses on the mechanics of how the user creates an event and how the program responds to the event. Naturally, all of this takes a bit of planning and arrangement. We need to tell Alice to listen for a particular kind of event and then what to do when the event happens. This means we need to write methods that describe the actions objects should take in response to an event.

We hope you will find that learning to use events is easy in Alice.

## 5-1 Interactive programming

### Control of flow

Writing an interactive program has one major difference from writing a non-interactive one (like the movies we wrote in the previous chapter). The difference is in how the sequence of actions is controlled. In a non-interactive program, the sequence of actions is pre-determined by the programmer. The programmer designs a complete storyboard and then writes the program

91

code for the animated actions. Once the program is constructed and tested, then every time the program runs, the same sequence of actions will occur. In an interactive program the sequence of actions is determined at runtime, when:

- The user clicks the mouse or presses a key on the keyboard.
- Objects in the scene move (randomly or guided by the user) to create some condition, such as a collision.

## Events

Each time the user clicks the mouse or presses a key, an event is generated that triggers a response. Objects in the scene may move to positions that trigger a response. Each time the program runs, different user interactions or different object actions may occur and the overall animation sequence may be different from some previous execution of the program. For example, in a video game that simulates a car race, where the player is "driving" a race car, the sequence of scenes is determined by whether the player is skillful in steering the car to stay on the road through twists, turns, and hazards that suddenly appear in the scene.

## Event handling methods

How do events affect what you do as an animation programmer? You must think about all possible events and make plans for what should happen—responses to the events. Animation methods are then written to carry out responses. Finally, the event must be linked to the responding method. The method is now said to be an event handling method.

When an event occurs and an event handling method is called, the location of objects in the scene may or may not be the same as the last time. This is because the user's actions may change the scene and the location of objects between calls to the event handling method.

## Keyboard-control example

We begin with an acrobatic air-show flight simulator. The initial scene, as illustrated in Figure 5-1-1, consists of the biplane (Vehicles) in midair and some objects on the ground (house, barn, and so forth from the Buildings and Farm folders). A guidance system will allow the user to be the pilot. The biplane has controls that allow the pilot to maneuver the plane forward, left, and right. We want to program the biplane to perform a popular show stunt—a barrel turn. In the exercises at the end of this Chapter, other stunts can be added.

**Figure 5-1-1.** Initial scene

### Input

The whole idea of a flight simulator is to allow the user to interact with the biplane. The user provides input that sends a signal to animate a particular motion, perhaps by pressing a set of keys on the keyboard. For example, arrow keys can be used, each corresponding to a given direction of movement. Of course, input can also be obtained from mouse clicks, the movement of a trackball, or the use of a game stick controller. In this text, we will rely on the keyboard and mouse to provide user input for interaction with the animations.

In our flight simulator, the arrow keys and spacebar will be used to provide input from the user. If the user presses the up arrow key, the biplane will move forward. If the user presses the left or right arrow keys, the biplane will turn left or right. For the acrobatic barrel turn, we will use the spacebar. The selection of these keys is arbitrary—other keys could easily be used.

### Design—storyboards

We are ready to design the flight simulator program—the set of instructions that tell Alice how to perform the animations. Each time the user presses an arrow key or the spacebar, an event is generated. The animation program consists of methods to respond to these events. To simplify the discussion, let's concentrate on two possible events: the spacebar press for the barrel turn and the up arrow key to move the biplane forward. Two storyboards are needed, as shown below. Note that sound is optional and can be omitted.

| | |
|---|---|
| **Event:** Spacebar press<br><br>**Response:**<br>  *Do together*<br>    roll biplane a full revolution<br>    play biplane engine sound | **Event:** Up arrow key press<br><br>**Response:**<br>  *Do together*<br>    move biplane forward<br>    play biplane engine sound |

### Methods to respond to the events

The only object affected by key-press events is the biplane, so the methods can be class-level methods for the biplane. Two methods will be written, *flyForward* and *barrel*. The *flyForward* method will handle an up arrow key-press event by moving the biplane forward as illustrated in Figure 5-1-2. The barrel method will handle a spacebar-press event by rolling the biplane

**Figure 5-1-2.** The *flyForward* method

one complete revolution, illustrated in Figure 5-1-3. In the methods shown here, a sound is played simultaneously with the movement. The duration of the biplane movement is set to be approximately the same as the length of the sound (in seconds). As noted previously, sound is a nice feature but can be omitted. If sound is used, the sound should be imported for the biplane. (Importing a sound file was introduced in Chapter 4, Section 2.)

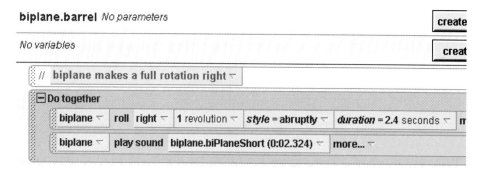

**Figure 5-1-3.** The *barrel* method

## Link events to methods

Each method must be linked to the event that will be used to trigger the method as a response. The Events editor is where links are created. The Events editor is shown in Figure 5-1-4. As you know, Alice creates a link between *When the world starts* (an event) and *World.my first method*, as shown in Figure 5-1-4.

**Figure 5-1-4.** Event editor

In the flight simulator, two events (the up arrow key press and the spacebar key press) need to be linked to their corresponding method (*flyForward* and *barrel*). First, create an event by clicking the **create new event** button and then selecting the event from the popup menu. In Figure 5-1-5, the *When a key is typed* event is selected.

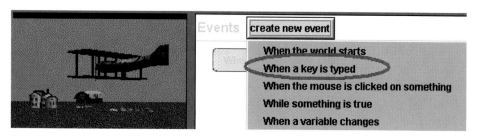

**Figure 5-1-5.** Creating a key-press event

In Figure 5-1-6, an event for *any key* pressed has been added to the Events editor. The "*any key*" and "*Nothing*" tiles are placeholders that need to be replaced. To tell Alice that we want to use the up arrow key, clicking on the *any key* tile and select *Up* from the popup menu.

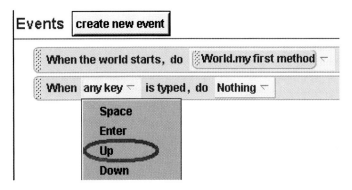

**Figure 5-1-6.** Specifying the up arrow key

Now that Alice has been notified that an up arrow key event may occur, we need to tell Alice what to do when the event happens. As shown in Figure 5-1-7, click on the *Nothing* tile and then select *biplane* and *flyForward* from the popup menu.

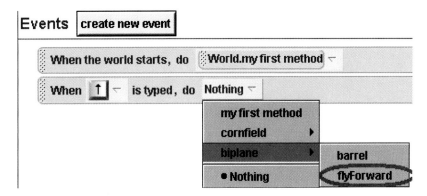

**Figure 5-1-7.** Link event-handling method to an event

The process is repeated to link the spacebar to the barrel method. Figure 5-1-8 shows the Events editor with both links completed.

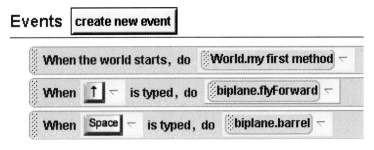

**Figure 5-1-8.** Links completed

## Testing

Now the world should be tested. To test the flight simulator, just save the world and press the **Play** button. Nothing happens until the up arrow is pressed, which causes the biplane to call its *flyForward* method.

Events and methods could be created for the left and right arrow keys, and other acrobatic stunts could be written. (See Exercise 1.) However, it is important to test event handling methods as they are developed. Write a method and test it, write a method and test it, until the program is completed. This is a recommended program development strategy called incremental development. Its advantage is in making it easier to debug your program. When something isn't working, it can be fixed before it causes problems elsewhere.

**Note:** An interactive world such as a flight simulator requires that the user know what keys to press to make the simulation work properly. A startup method could be written in *World.my first method* to display 3D text or a billboard for a quick explanation of the guidance system. After a few seconds, the 3D text (or billboard) can be made to disappear (by setting its *isShowing* property to *false*), and then the simulation can begin. 3D text and billboards were described in Tips & Techniques 2.

## Tips & Techniques 5
### Events

 **A Quick Reference to Events**

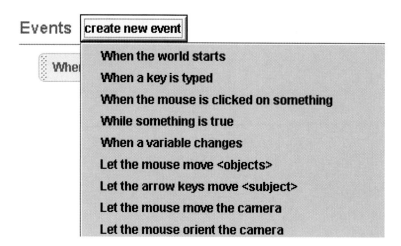

**Figure T-5-1.** Possible events in Alice

- *When the world starts.* This event happens once, when the Play button is first pressed and the Alice world begins to run.

- *When a key is typed.* This allows for a method to be called in response to the user pressing one of the keys on the keyboard.

- *When the mouse is clicked on something.* Each time the mouse is clicked on an object in the world, a method is called to handle the event.

- *While something is true.* While some condition is rue, perform the action in the called method.

- *When a variable changes.* This event allows for calling a method every time a specified property of an object changes value.

- *Let the mouse move objects.* This event automatically calls an internal Alice method that moves the object in a drag-and-drop manner.

- *Let the arrow keys move <subject>.* This allows the user to move a specified object by pressing the arrow keys. The up arrow moves the object forward, down arrow backward, the right and left arrows move the object right and left.

- *Let the mouse move the camera.* This allows the user to "steer" the camera with the mouse during an animation. Note that it is possible to point the camera away from the animation. If this happens, you will no longer see what is going on.

- *Let the mouse orient the camera.* Like the preceding event, this one must be used with caution, as you can easily orient the camera to point into space and then miss the rest of the animation that is running.

## Exercises

### 5-1 Exercises

1. *Flight Simulator Completion*

   (a) Create the world for the biplane acrobatic air-show example as presented in this section. Implement the *flyForward* and *barrel* event handling methods and link them to the corresponding events. Make the move and roll actions have an abrupt style to reduce the pause in the animation between key presses. If your computer has sound, use a biplane sound to make the animation more realistic.

   (b) When you have the *flyForward* and *barrel* methods working, add *flyLeft* and *flyRight* event handling methods for the left and right arrow keys to steer the biplane left or right.

   (c) Add a *forwardLoop* stunt that works when the user presses the Enter key.

2. *Robot Remote Control*

   The world for this exercise is similar to the FirstEncounter world in Chapters 2 through 4. In this world, however, we want to allow the user to control the robot using some sort of remote control. One possibility is to use the TwoButton switch (Controls) to simulate a robot control system. When the user clicks the green button on the switch, the robot should move forward, with two of its legs providing a walking motion. When the user clicks the red button on the switch, the robot should move backward, with two different legs walking in the opposite direction. Use the world-level function *ask the user for a number* to allow the user to determine how many meters the robot moves forward or backward.

3. *Typing Tutor*

   Learning to type rapidly (without looking at the keyboard) is a skill requiring much practice. In this exercise, you are to create a typing tutor that encourages the beginning typist to type a specific set of letters. Use 3D text letters (3D Text folder) to create a word in the world, (for example, you could create the word ALICE with the letters A, L, I, C, and E) and create a method for each letter that spins the letter two times. When the user types a letter key on the keyboard that matches the letter on the screen, the letter on the screen should perform its spin method. Also include an additional method, *spinWord*, which spins all the letters when the user presses the spacebar.

**Hint:** Use *asSeenBy* to spin the word.

4. *Rotational Motion*

A popular topic in Physics is the study of rotational motion. Create a world with at least four objects (such as a compass, mailbox, mantleClock, and tire.) Create a realistic rotation method for each object that has the object rotate 1 full revolution and then perform some other action. For example, if one of your objects is a compass, make the compass needle spin around quickly in one direction and then spin around again in the opposite direction. Add events that will call the rotational motion method for an object when the object is clicked. (If the world has four objects, four events will be needed.)

5. *Ninja Motion*

A ninja (EvilNinja in People folder) is trying out for a karate movie, and he needs a little practice. Create a world with a ninja object in a dojo. The motions the ninja needs to practice are: jump, duck, chop, and kick. If you have not already done so, (see Exercise 12 in Chapter 4), write motion methods for the ninja that include the following:

>  *kickRight*, *kickLeft:* allows the ninja to kick his right/left leg, including all appropriate movements (e.g., foot turning, etc.)

>  *rightJab*, *leftJab:* allows the ninja to do a jabbing motion with his right/left arms

Create events and event handling methods that provide the user with controls to make the ninja jump, duck, jab, and kick.

6. *The Cheshire Cat*

Consider the Cheshire cat (Animals) from the *Alice in Wonderland* books. Sometimes, the cat would disappear, leaving only his grin. At other times, the cat would reappear.

Create such a world, where the cat (except for its smile) disappears when the red button of the switch (Controls) is clicked, then reappears when the green button is clicked. (The tree is found in the Nature folder.)

7. *Turtle Motion Control (challenging)*

In this project, you are to create a turtle motion controller to help the turtle (Animals) perform exercises for his upcoming race with the rabbit. Create a world that contains only a turtle and then create motion control methods for the turtle:

> ***headBob:*** allows the turtle's head to bob a little
>
> ***tailWag:*** allows the turtle's tail to wag
>
> ***oneStep:*** allows the turtle to move forward one step; his legs should move while he is taking that one step
>
> ***walkForward:*** combines the above three methods, to make a realistic step; all movements should take the same amount of time and occur at the same time
>
> ***turnAround:*** turns the turtle 180 degrees; he should be walking while turning
>
> ***turnLeft, turnRight:*** turns the turtle left/right, walking while he is turning

Create keyboard controls:

> When the up arrow key is pressed, the turtle is to walk forward.
>
> When the down arrow key is pressed, the turtle is to turn around.
>
> When the left arrow key is pressed, the turtle is to turn left.
>
> When the right arrow key is pressed, the turtle is to turn right.

Test the turtle motion control system by running your world and trying all the interactions at least once.

## Summary

The focus of this chapter was the creation of interactive (event-driven) worlds. Creating worlds with events will allow you to build significantly more interesting worlds such as game-like animations and simulations. In many object-oriented programming languages, event-driven programming requires knowledge of advanced topics. The Events editor allows you to create events and link them to event handling methods. The event handling method has the responsibility of taking action each time the event occurs. The Events editor handles many of the messy details of event-driven programming.

## Important concepts in this chapter

- An event is something that happens.
- An event is created by user input (keyboard press, mouse click, joystick movement).
- An event is linked to an event handling method.
- Each time an event occurs, its corresponding event handling method is called. This is what is meant by event-driven programming.
- The event handling method contains instructions to carry out a response to the event.

# Appendices

# Appendix A

## Using Alice

The purpose of this tutorial-style self-paced exercise is to help you learn the basics of using Alice. We suggest you work through these exercises with a friend. You'll have fun together, and you'll be able to help each other work through any parts you might find confusing. If at any point you get lost or stuck, go back to the beginning of the section, reload the world and try again. You can't hurt anything and you will lose only a few minutes of work.

### Part 1: Running virtual worlds in alice

In this part, you will work with two worlds (FirstWorld and DancingBee—found on the CD that accompanies this text). You will also create and save your own new world.

**Whenever you see text printed like this, specific instructions are given about what to do.**

How to Start Alice: Alice can be started in one of two ways:

1. **Click the icon on the desktop of your machine. (See Figure A-1-1 on next page.)**

2. **Or, use the windows search utility to find and click on the "Alice.exe" startup file.**

Alice may take a minute or two to load.

In some installations, the Alice startup may display a choice dialog box, shown in Figure A-1-2. If you decide you no longer wish to see this dialog box each time you start Alice, uncheck the box in the lower left corner of the dialog box, labeled "Show this dialog at start." (Note: Some academic computer network systems restore each computer to a primary image with a reboot. We advise that you do not uncheck the box if your computer is part of a network system.)

**Click on the Templates tab and select a "grass" world as the initial scene. Then, click on Open.** Alice starts with an empty world. In the World View window, you should see the green grass and blue sky initial scene, shown in Figure A-1-3. If this is not the case, consult the instructions at www.alice.org on how to troubleshoot your installation of Alice.

### World 1: A first animation

Let's start by opening a world.

**Select the File menu at the top of the Alice window and then choose Open World as shown in Figure A-1-4.**

Alice opens a dialog box for opening a world file. **Click the Textbook tab to view text examples, as shown in Figure A-1-5.**

Alice

**Figure A-1-1.** Alice shorcut icon on the desktop of your computer

**Figure A-1-2.** Startup dialog box

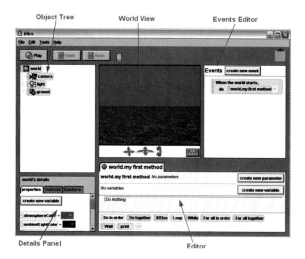

**Figure A-1-3.** The Alice interface

**Figure A-1-4.** File open world menu

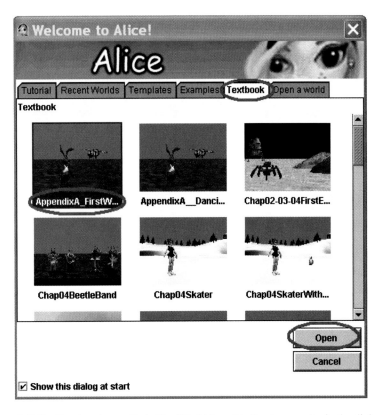

**Figure A-1-5.** Opening AppendixA_FirstWorld from Textbook examples in the dialog box

**Select AppendixA_FirstWorld and click the Open button.** The bee and hare objects are displayed in the world that opens, as shown in Figure A-1-6. The Object tree lists the objects in the world.

**Click Play to run the world.**

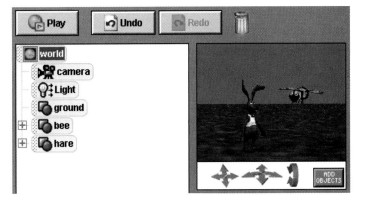

**Figure A-1-6.  Play** button at top, Object tree on left, First World initial scene on right

Take a close look at the controls at the top of the animation window (Figure A-1-7). Some buttons, such as **Pause** and **Restart,** are obvious. The **Take Picture** button will take a single snapshot of the animation and save it as a graphic image file. (A popup menu allows selection of a location for saving the file.) The **Speed** slide control allows you to adjust the speed of the animation.

**Figure A-1-7.** The animation window

Of course, the speed of the animation is affected by the capabilities of your computer hardware. A helpful hint is that the size of the window in which the animation runs (the **World Running** window) affects the speed of an animation. If your animation is running too slowly, make the window smaller. (Grab the lower right corner of the window with the mouse and drag the window to the size you want.) After the window size is changed, Alice will remember it the next time you play an animation.

**Close the animation window for the FirstWorld (use a mouse-click on the X at the upper right of the animation window or click the Stop button).**

## World 2

World 1 (FirstWorld) is a "movie" style of animation. A movie runs from beginning to end while you, as the human "user," view the animation. Let's look at a world that is interactive where you can make choices as to how the animation works.

**Use File → Open World to open the dialog box.**
**In the dialog box, select Textbook and then AppendixA_Dancing Bee, as shown in Figure A-1-8.**
**Click Play.**
Then, try each of the two choices (keys can be pressed in any order):

1. Press the up arrow key
2. Press the space bar

**When you have finished viewing the animation, close the window.**
This world uses the same initial scene as in the first world, viewed above, but the program has been changed to be an interactive, event-driven animation. Pressing the up arrow key creates an event. Alice responds to the up arrow event by making the hare jump. Pressing the space bar creates a different event. Alice responds to the space bar event by making the bee perform a pirouette in flight. This world is an example of an interactive, event-driven animation.

## Summary

Here's a recap of what we just covered with Worlds 1 and 2. If you're not comfortable with any of these topics, go back to the start of this section and go through it again.

**Figure A-1-8.** Select AppendixA_Dancing Bee world

- How to **Start** Alice
- How to **Open** a saved world
- How to **Play** a world
- How to **Stop** a world
- Running interactive worlds with events and responses

## World 3: Creating and saving your own new world

**Figure A-1-9.** Select New World from the File menu.

**Click on the File menu in the upper left-hand corner of Alice. Select "New World" as shown in Figure A-1-9. Then select the snow template for an initial scene.**

### Saving a world

Each time a new world is created, it is a good idea to save the world. Then, if the computer crashes or loses power (it can happen, even on the best of machines!), your work will be safe to reload when the computer is rebooted. A world can be saved to any one of several different locations (desktop, file server space, disk, or a memory stick). If a disk is to be used, we recommend that a zip disk or memory stick be used rather than a floppy disk (the size of the world may be more than a floppy disk can hold). The example below shows directories on a zip disk, but other storage devices should work just as well.

**Go to File → Save World As.**

This brings up a Save World dialog box that lets you navigate to the location where the world will be saved, as shown in Figure A-1-10.

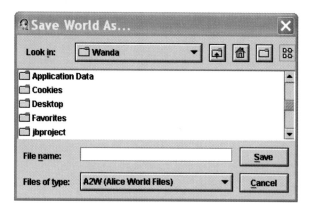

**Figure A-1-10.** Save World dialog box

**Navigate to the folder (directory) where you plan to save your world, as shown in Figure A-1-11.** We recommend that you create a folder named **AliceWorlds** where you will save all your animations.

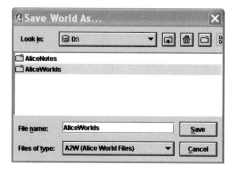

**Figure A-1-11.** Select a folder where the world be saved

Make up a name for your world—we recommend a single word name, such as SnowmanExercise, that uses upper- and lowercase characters. **Enter the name for your world and then click the Save button, as shown in Figure A-1-12.**

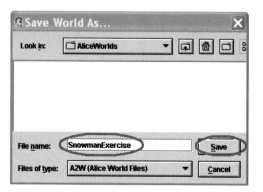

**Figure A-1-12.** Enter a file name and click **save**

Your world will be saved with the **.a2w** extension (an Alice version 2 world).

As you work on your world, Alice will periodically prompt you to save your world. We recommend that you save the world every half hour or so. Alice automatically makes back-up copies of your world when you save it. The folder is named **"Backups of ...."**

## Adding objects to the world

**Click on the Add Objects button in the lower right of the World view window, as shown in Figure A-1-13.**

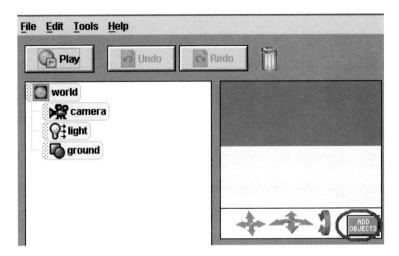

**Figure A-1-13.**  Add Objects button

Alice opens the Scene Editor. A visual directory to the Local and Web Galleries is provided for access to 3D models. A **Search Gallery** button allows you to search for a particular kind of object. (See Appendix B for more details on searching for an object.)

> **Important Note:** The Local Gallery is a sampler, containing an assortment of 3D models. The CD and Web galleries contain thousand of models. See the next section of this tutorial for instructions on how to use the Web Gallery. The CD Gallery folder will only be displayed if the Alice CD is in your machine. Examples, exercises, and projects in this text use 3D models from both the Local Gallery and the Web Gallery. If you are looking for a particular model in the Local Gallery and cannot find it, try looking in the online Web Gallery at www.alice.org.

**Click on the Local Gallery folder, as shown in Figure A-1-14.**

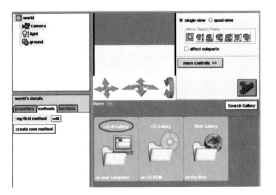

**Figure A-1-14.**  Local Gallery folder

**Note:** The Gallery is organized into collections—for example Animals, Buildings, and People.

**Click on the people thumbnail picture, as shown in Figure A-1-15.**

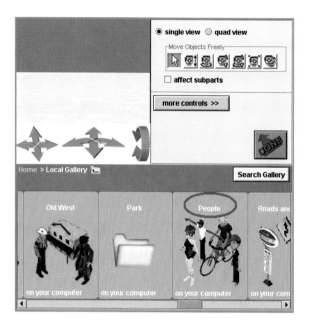

**Figure A-1-15.** The People collection of 3D models

**Click on the Snowman.**

**Click add instance to world. You can also add an object to the world by using the mouse to drag and drop the object into the world, as shown in Figure A-1-16.**

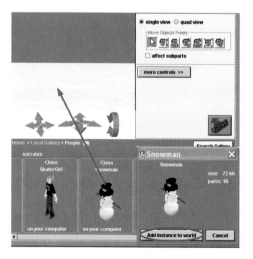

**Figure A-1-16.** Two options: drag and drop or click to add an an object (instance)

**Note:** Drag and drop works relative to the ground. If the ground is deleted from a world, the drag and drop technique cannot be used to add an object to the world.

### Using the web gallery (optional)

If your computer is attached to the internet, you may wish to use the Web Gallery, as shown in Figure A-1-17. The online gallery provides many more models than are available in the Local Gallery.

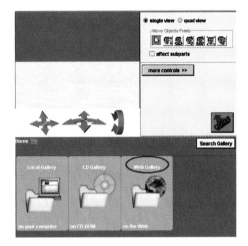

**Figure A-1-17.**  The Web Gallery folder

**Note:** The models in the Web Gallery may take longer than the models on the CD to load, depending on the speed of your connection.

**Follow the same procedure as outlined above to add a snowman object from the online People collection of 3D models.**

### Mouse controls in the scene editor

**Drag the snowman around the scene with the mouse. Then click Undo, as shown in Figure A-1-18.**

**Figure A-1-18.**  The Undo button

This illustrates an important point—you don't have to worry about messing things up. Use Undo to get back to a previous position.

On the far right of the scene editor is a toolkit of buttons that allow you to select the way the mouse moves an object in 3D space. By default, the horizontal (left-right, forward-back) movement is selected.

**One at a time, select each of the mouse control buttons and experiment with the snowman using that control, as shown in Figure A-1-19.**

For your reference, Figure A-1-20 identifies the actions of the mouse control buttons. The default button, labeled "Horizontal," allows the mouse to move an object left, right, forward, or back in the scene.

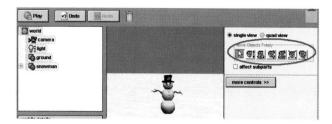

**Figure A-1-19.** Mouse control toolkit.

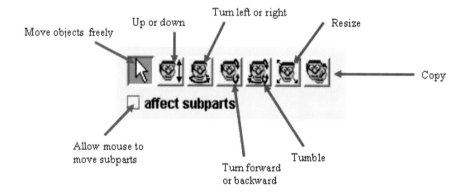

**Figure A-1-20.** Mouse control buttons

## Moving subparts of objects

The mouse movement controls are automatically set to move an entire object. If you check the **affect subparts** box, the mouse can be used to control the movement of subparts, rather than the entire object.

Check the "affect subparts" box and use the vertical mouse control to move the snowman's hat, as shown in Figure A-1-21.

**Figure A-1-21.** Affect subparts is checked

**Be sure to uncheck the "affect subparts" box before going on!**

## Experiment with the copy and delete:

1. **Use the Copy mouse control button (see mouse control reference above) to create a second snowman. Then, click on the snowman.** This creates a second snowman object (in the same location).

2. Actually, a copy is somewhat like a ghost of the original object—not completely independent. In most worlds, we prefer to add new objects. **Delete the second snowman— right-click on the second snowman and choose Delete from the popup menu.**

3. **Finally, click the mouse cursor in the mouse control buttons to stop copying objects.**

**Note:** If the ground is deleted in a world, new objects can only be added using the "Add instance" button (rather than a drag-and-drop action).

**Add a snowwoman object to the world.**

The world will now have two objects, a snowman and a snowwoman, as shown in Figure A-1-22.

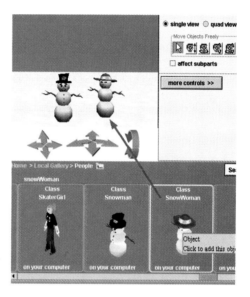

**Figure A-1-22.** Snowman and snowwoman

## Using quad view

We would like the snowman and snowwoman to stand side-by-side and face one another. The scene editor can be used to arrange the two objects.

**Select "quad view" in the editor, as shown in Figure A-1-23.**

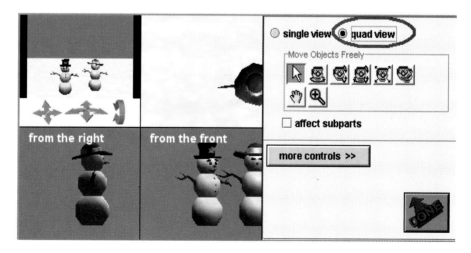

**Figure A-1-23.** Quad view panes

The world view window changes to a four-pane **quad view.** The four panes show Camera, Top, Right and Front viewpoints. Note that the vertical mouse control button is no longer available because the **Front** and **Right** panes automatically have vertical movement. The toolbox now displays a second row of mouse control buttons, containing a scroll and a zoom button, as labeled in Figure A-1-24.

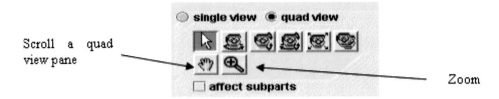

**Figure A-1-24.** A second row of mouse controls

In the quad view shown above, the snowwoman is partially out of sight in the Top view. (Your world may appear somewhat different than ours.) The scroll tool can be used to reposition the viewpoint in a pane. As shown in Figure A-1-25, we used the scroll control to reposition the Top view pane.

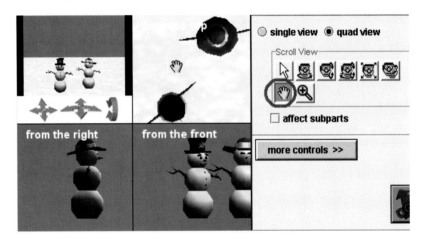

**Figure A-1-25.** Using the scroll tool

Another useful feature is the zoom tool. The zoom tool can be used to zoom in or out in a pane. As shown in Figure A-1-26, we have used the zoom tool to zoom out in the pane that shows the view from the top.

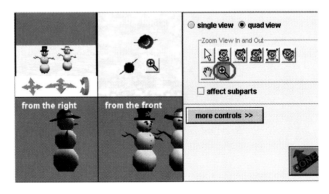

**Figure A-1-26.** Using the zoom tool

**Use the mouse to arrange the two objects side-by-side.**

A side-by-side position can be recognized when one object (more or less) hides the other in the Right view (see circled Right view pane in the Figure A-1-27).

**Figure A-1-27.** Right view pane

**Use the mouse to arrange the objects facing one another.**

The facing position is recognized in the Top and Front views, as shown in Figure A-1-28.

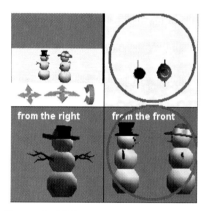

**Figure A-1-28.** Top and Front view panes

Click **single view** to return to a single pane in the scene editor, as shown in Figure A-1-29.

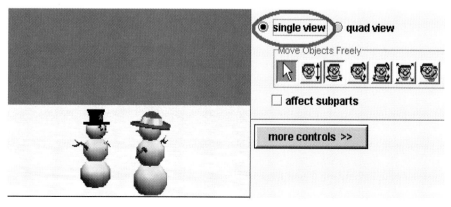

**Figure A-1-29.** Single view

### Using ctrl and shift keys with mouse-object movement

Although the mouse control buttons offer several options for moving and posing objects in a scene, it is sometimes more convenient to use keyboard controls with the mouse. Pressing and holding-down the Ctrl key allows you to use the mouse to turn an object around in a spinning motion. Pressing and holding-down the Shift key allows you to use the mouse to move an object up and down.

### Moving the camera

In setting up a scene, the camera viewpoint allows us to adjust what the user will be able to see in the animation. It may be helpful to think of the camera as a remote-controlled airborne device that hovers in mid-air over the scene. By moving the camera, we change our view of the world.

The blue controls at the bottom of the scene editor window are the camera controls, as shown in Figure A-1-30.

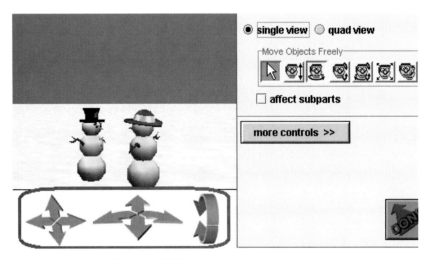

**Figure A-1-30.** Camera navigation controls

**Click and drag on the camera controls to get an idea of what each camera control does.**

You can always use Undo to return to a previous camera position.

### Arranging many objects in an initial scene

When many objects are to be in the scene, adding objects one at a time and arranging them around the scene can be time consuming. The reason is that not only are you moving objects, you are also moving the camera around the scene. After several such moves, a new object might not be in view of the camera when it is first added to the scene. This means you may spend a lot of time with the camera controls trying to find newly added objects and arranging objects in the scene.

We recommend that all objects for the world be added to the scene immediately upon creating the world. Then use the mouse and camera controls to arrange objects in the scene. This simple process saves a lot of time and makes setting up the initial scene much easier. Figure A-1-31(a) on the next page shows a new world where many objects have been added, all clustered near the center of the world. Figure A-1-31(b) shows the objects rearranged in the scene.

## Summary

Here's a recap of what you just learned with World 3. If you're not comfortable with any of these topics, go back to the beginning of this section and try it again.

**Figure A-1-31.** (a) All objects near center of world (b) Objects rearranged in the scene

- How to make a new world
- Saving a world
- Adding objects to the world
- Using mouse controls (in the scene editor)
- Using mouse controls for subparts of objects
- Deleting an object
- Using quad view
- Camera movement
- Arranging objects in a scene

## Part 2: Using popup menus to create an initial scene

In Part 1, you used mouse controls to arrange objects in a scene. In this part, you will learn how to use methods to work with objects in setting up a scene.

Alice provides a number of built-in instructions that can be used to adjust the size and position of objects in a scene. These instructions are called methods. To illustrate their use, let's work with a new world where methods will be used to set up the scene (in addition to the mouse controls you learned to use in Part 1 of this Appendix).

**To begin this section, first use** File → New **World to start a new world. Select the grass template world. Click on the Add Objects button to set up your initial scene, as shown in Figure A-2-1.**

**Add a happy tree and a frog to the new world.**

The frog can be found in the Animals folder of the Local Gallery. The happy tree is in the Nature folder.

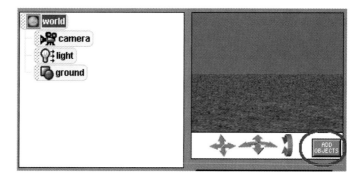

**Figure A-2-1.** Add Objects button

As seen in the Figure A-2-2, the frog is a bit small and it seems to fade into the grass, making it somewhat difficult to see. This situation is great for camouflaging the frog from its enemies but is not so good for an animation. You can use a *resize* method to make the frog larger.

**Figure A-2-2.** The frog is too small

**Right-click on *frog* in the Object tree.**
**Select the method "*frog resize*" and select 2 as the amount as shown in Figure A-2-3.**
This will make the frog 2 times as big as its current size.

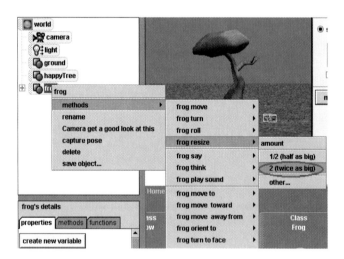

**Figure A-2-3.** Resize the frog, twice as big

**Note:** Resizing an object may have some unexpected results. An object standing on the ground may sink into the ground. **Reposition the object using the mouse, as needed.**

The *turn* method makes an object turn in a given direction (forward, back, left, right) by a given amount (in revolutions). An object moves relative to its own sense of direction (orientation).
**Use a method to turn the frog left 1/4 revolution, as shown in Figure A-2-4.**
The *roll* method rolls an object left or right.
**Use a roll method to roll the tree left 1/4 revolution, as shown in Figure A-2-5.**
The *stand up* instruction makes an object's vertical axis line up with the vertical axis of the world. In other words, the object stands up!
**Use a stand up instruction to put the tree back into an upright position, as shown in Figure A-2-6.**

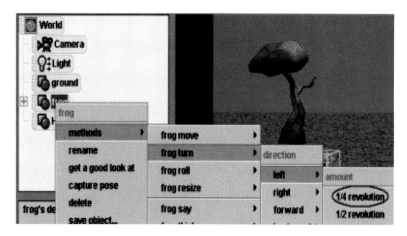

**Figure A-2-4.**  Turn the frog left 1/4 revolution

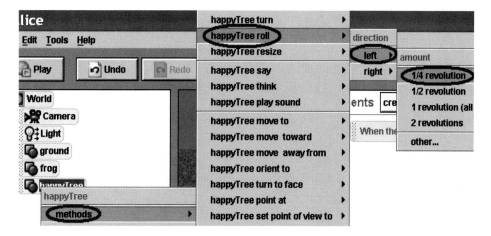

**Figure A-2-5.**  Roll the happyTree left 1/4 revolution

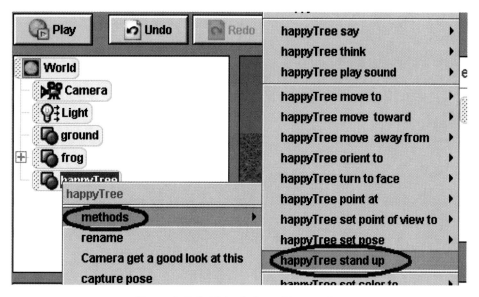

**Figure A-2-6.**  Make the happyTree stand up

The *turn to face* method makes an object turn to look toward another object. **Use turn to face to make the frog face the tree, as shown in Figure A-2-7.**

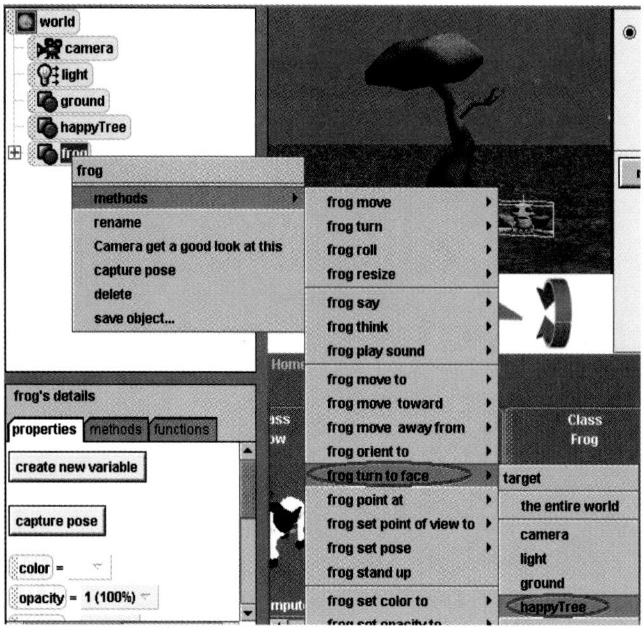

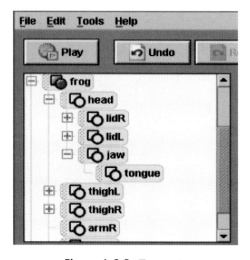

**Figure A-2-7.**  The frog turns to face the happyTree

## Using methods with object subparts

Subparts of an object can be manipulated with a method, by clicking on the subpart in the Object tree and then right-clicking the subpart to get the popup menu. **To view a list of the subparts of an object, first left-click on the plus box to the immediate left of the object in the Object tree.** Figure A-2-8 shows the frog's subparts in the expanded Object tree. One of the frog's parts is its jaw—and the tongue is a subpart of the jaw. (Parts can have parts, which can have parts, and so on ....)

**Select the frog tongue and a method to move the tongue forward "Other" amount, as shown in Figure A-2-9.** A number pad pops up where you can select the amount. **Enter .05.** (This is an arbitrary value—try different values until you get a satisfactory effect.)

**Figure A-2-8.**  Frog parts

The frog sticks its tongue out, as shown in Figure A-2-10.

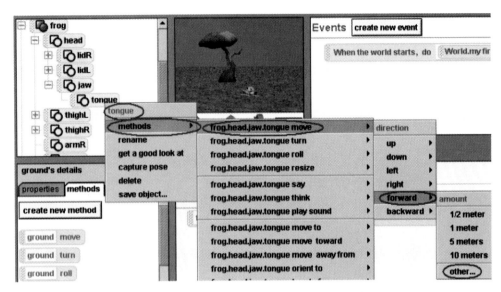

**Figure A-2-9.**  Move the frog's tongue forward

**Figure A-2-10.**  The frog's tongue sticks out

## Get a good look at this object

The right-click popup menu for an object displays a menu containing several items. In this tutorial, you have used *methods*. Other menu items (*rename, capture pose*, and *save object*) are explained, as needed, in example programs in the text. One item in the menu is different from others in the menu. The *methods, rename, capture pose, delete*, and *save object* items are all designed to act on the object. But, *Camera get a look at this* is a camera method. When you select *Camera get a good look at this* from the menu, the camera zooms in to display a close-up view of an object. You can use Undo to return to the previous view.

**Use *"Camera get a good look at this"* to get a close-up view of the frog, as shown in Figure A-2-11.**

(If another object is between the camera and the object, and blocks the camera view, use Undo and move the camera or the object.)

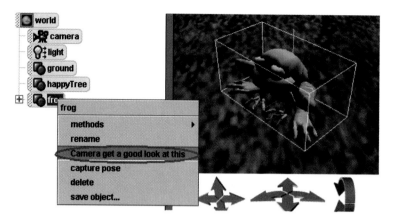

**Figure A-2-11.** *Camera get a good look at this*

## A comparison of motion controls

In Part 1 of this tutorial, you experimented with mouse motion controls. In Part 2, you worked with methods. In both cases, you were positioning objects to set up an initial world scene. You may be wondering, "Which kind of motion control is best—mouse controls or methods?"

We have found that mouse motion control (in the scene editor) is very good for placing an object in an approximate location, but the popup menu methods are needed for exact alignment. The scene editor (especially the quad view) is great for positioning objects relative to one another. It is quite easy to add an object to a world and then use the mouse to move and rotate it approximately to the location we would like. If we make a mistake, we can simply undo our actions (or even delete the object) and try again. While the approximate positioning of an object is easy to do with the mouse, its exact positioning (we find) is a bit more challenging. For example, trying to position one object on top of another is difficult to do with the mouse. Getting them approximately on top of one another isn't too difficult, but placing them exactly is tough to do with the mouse. Methods, however, give good alignment. In setting up world scenes, the best strategy is to use a combination of methods and mouse motion controls.

# Appendix B

## Managing the Alice Interface

### Searching the gallery

Often, you may want to find an object, say a ball, but not know where to find the 3D model for it in the gallery. You can search the gallery for a particular kind of object. **Click the Search Gallery button, as shown in Figure B-1-1.**

You can search either your Local Gallery or the Web gallery at www.alice.org (assuming your computer is connected to the internet). You should always search your Local Gallery first, since this search will be much faster. **When the search prompt is displayed, as in Figure B-1-2, enter the name of the model (or part of the name) you are searching for, and then click on the Search! button next to the text box.**

If you do not find what you are looking for, you search www.alice.org, as illustrated in Figure B-1-3. The first time you search www.alice.org, your search may take a couple of minutes (depending on the speed of your internet connection). Additional searches will be much faster.

### Creating your own people models

The galleries provide over a thousand 3D models for use in building your worlds. Alice is not a graphics model builder, but two special people-building utilities (hebuilder and shebuilder) are available in the People folder of the local gallery, as seen in Figure B-1-4. **A click on hebuilder or shebuilder will bring up a people builder window (Figure B-1-5), where you**

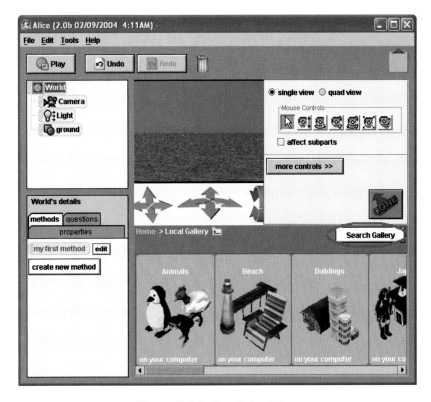

**Figure B-1-1.** Search the Gallery

**Figure B-1-2.** Entering a name for an object

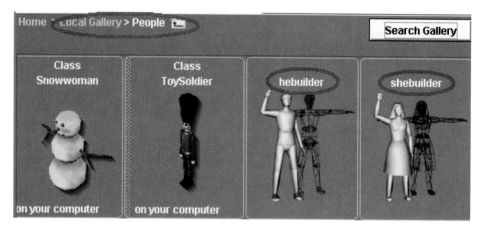

**Figure B-1-3.** Search the Web gallery at www.alice.org

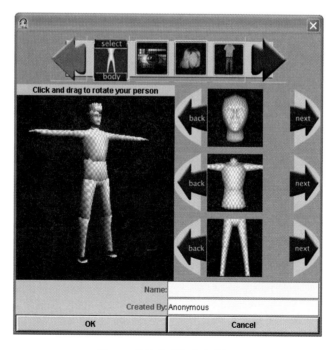

**Figure B-1-4.** The hebuilder and shebuilder model building utilities

**Figure B-1-5.** The hebuider

can select the desired body type, hair, skin color, eyes, and clothing. When you have completed your selections, click on OK to name the object and add it to your world. Alice automatically defines a *walk* method for the person object that you build. This is an advantage, because a *walk* method is difficult to write on your own.

## Copy and paste: clipboards

Suppose a particular sequence of animation instructions is something that you would like to copy and paste. This is where a clipboard is useful. **To copy a sequence of instructions, click on the left side (on the small dots) of the block of instructions you would like copied.** This action selects the instructions to be copied. (Note: Selecting a *Do in order* or a *Do together* statement selects all the instructions within it.) **Then use the mouse to drag the instructions to the clipboard.** Figure B-1-6 illustrates dragging instructions onto the clipboard from the editor.

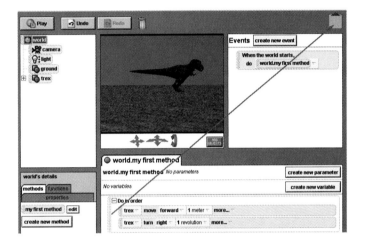

**Figure B-1-6.** Dragging instructions to the clipboard

Once instructions have been copied to a clipboard, the clipboard changes color (white). The color change is a visual clue indicating that copied instructions are now on the clipboard. **Now that the clipboard contains instructions, you can use the mouse to drag the selected instructions from the clipboard into the editor to create a new copy of those instructions elsewhere in your program, as illustrated in Figure B-1-7.** You now have two copies of the instructions in the editor. (You can delete the old instructions by dragging them to the waste basket.)

Note that a clipboard can hold only one set of instructions at a time. If instructions were previously copied to the clipboard, copying a new set of instructions to the same clipboard will overwrite (destroy) what was already there. As originally installed, Alice displays only one clipboard. The number of clipboards can be increased by selecting the **Edit** menu and then the **Preferences** menu item. In the **Seldom Used** tab of the Preferences window, modify the number of clipboards, as in Figure B-1-8.

## Deleting code

What if you make a mistake or want to change some code that you have created? The easiest way to remove a line of code is to **drag it to the wastebasket at the top of the Alice window.** An entire block of code can be deleted by dragging the block to the wastebasket, as illustrated in Figure B-1-9.

If you want to remove a *Do together* or *Do in order* block but keep the lines of code, **right click on the block and select *dissolve*, as seen in Figure B-1-10.** The lines of code

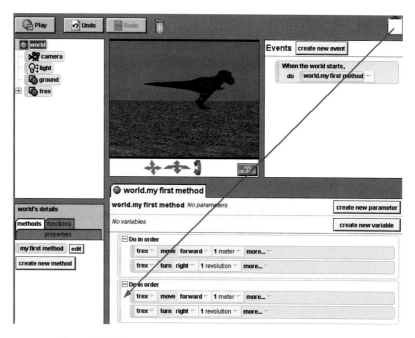

**Figure B-1-7.** Drag instructions from the clipboard into the editor

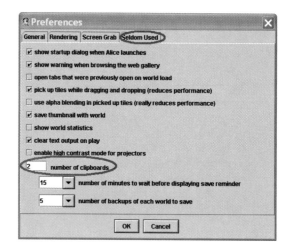

**Figure B-1-8.** Increasing the number of clipboards

will be promoted one level and the previously enclosing block will be erased, as shown in Figure B-1-11.

## Printing: Exporting program code to an HTML file

You may wish to print the code from one or more of your program methods. First, be sure the world is open in Alice. **Then, to print a method from your program, click on the File menu and select the Export Code For Printing menu item, as shown in Figure B-1-12. In the Print dialog box, select the name of the method (or methods) to be printed, the folder where the document is to be stored, and your name.** Then click the **Export Code** button, as illustrated in Figure B-1-13. The code in the selected methods will be exported to an HTML document, which can be printed from your browser.

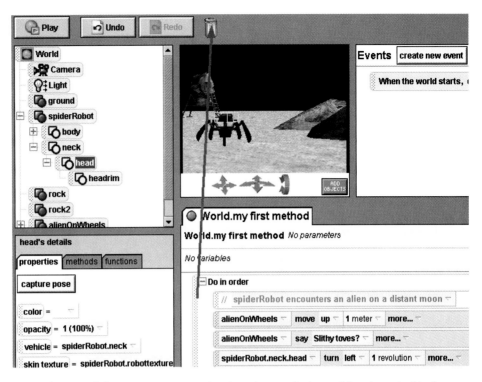

**Figure B-1-9.**  Dragging a block of code to the wastebasket to delete the entire block

**Figure B-1-10.**  Selecting *dissolve* to remove the *Do together* block

**Figure B-1-11.**  After *dissolve*, the *Do together* block has been erased but the instructions remain

**Figure B-1-12.** Selecting the *Export Code For Printing* menu item

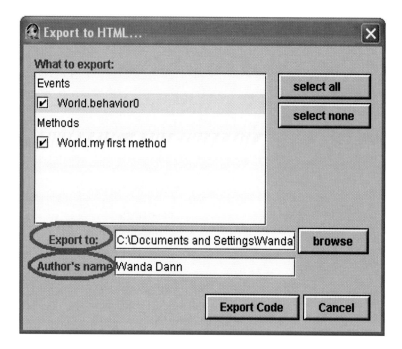

**Figure B-1-13.** Selecting a method to export for printing

## Web display: Exporting a world

Exporting a world for display on a Web page is an excellent way to show off your creativity. First be sure the world is open in Alice. **To export a world, click the File menu and then select the Export As A Web Page menu item, illustrated in Figure B-1-14.**

A **Save World for the Web** dialog box allows the entry of a title, width and height of the world window to be displayed in a browser, and a location where the Web files will be saved, as illustrated in Figure B-1-15. (The location in the Save Location box cannot be a URL.) A click on the Save button causes Alice to save three files to the directory you select: the usual .a2w file, an .html file, and a Java archive (.jar) file.

To allow others to view your world via the Internet, you must store the three files on a Web server. All three files must be in the same directory. The first time someone downloads a page, it will take a few seconds (depending on the speed of their Internet connection) because of the size

**Figure B-1-14.** Selecting the *Export As A Web Page* menu item

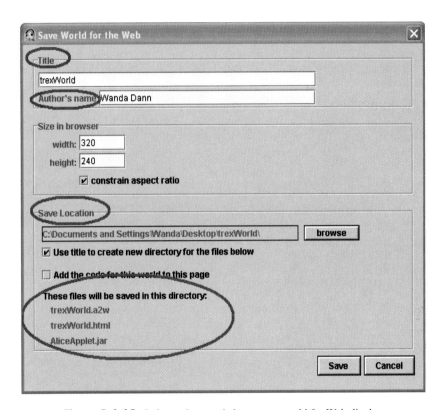

**Figure B-1-15.** Information needed to save a world for Web display

of the Java archive file. (If the computer does not have a Java enabled browser or Java 3D or Java Media Frameworks, the web page will prompt the user to download a plug-in from the Java website, maintained by *Sun Microsystems*®). Thereafter, a page will download quickly.

## Export to movie

At the time of this publication, this feature has not yet been implemented. We expect it may be implemented by the time you are reading this book. Check the www.alice.org website for updates.

# Index